OCCASIONAL PAPER 256

Moving to Greater Exchange Rate Flexibility
Operational Aspects Based on Lessons from Detailed Country Experiences

Inci Ötker-Robe and David Vávra, and a team of economists

INTERNATIONAL MONETARY FUND
Washington DC
2007

Production: IMF Multimedia Services Division
Typesetting: Alicia Etchebarne-Bourdin
Figures: Bob Lunsford

Ötker, Inci.
    Moving to greater exchange rate flexibility : operational aspects based
on lessons from detailed country experiences / Inci Ötker-Robe and David
Vávra, and a team consisting of Luis Ahumada . . . [et al.]. — Washington,
DC : International Monetary Fund, 2007.
        p. cm. — (Occasional paper ; 256)

    Includes bibliographical references.
    ISBN 978-1-58906-624-3

    1. Foreign exchange administration — Case studies.   2. Foreign
exchange rates — Case studies.   3. Monetary policy — Case
studies.   I. Vávra, David, 1972–   II. International Monetary
Fund.   III. Occasional paper (International Monetary Fund) ; no. 256
HG3851 .O854 2007

Price: US$30.00
(US$28.00 to full-time faculty members and
students at universities and colleges)

Please send orders to:
International Monetary Fund, Publication Services
700 19th Street, N.W., Washington, D.C. 20431, U.S.A.
Tel.: (202) 623-7430   Telefax: (202) 623-7201
E-mail: publications@imf.org
Internet: http://www.imf.org

Contents

2-6-07 International Monetary Fund 27.00 (–)

The following conventions are used in this publication:

- In tables, a blank cell indicates "not applicable," ellipsis points (. . .) indicate "not available," and 0 or 0.0 indicates "zero" or "negligible." Minor discrepancies between sums of constituent figures and totals are due to rounding.

- An en dash (–) between years or months (for example, 2005–06 or January–June) indicates the years or months covered, including the beginning and ending years or months; a slash or virgule (/) between years or months (for example, 2005/06) indicates a fiscal or financial year, as does the abbreviation FY (for example, FY2006).

- "Billion" means a thousand million; "trillion" means a thousand billion.

- "Basis points" refer to hundredths of 1 percentage point (for example, 25 basis points are equivalent to ¼ of 1 percentage point).

As used in this publication, the term "country" does not in all cases refer to a territorial entity that is a state as understood by international law and practice. As used here, the term also covers some territorial entities that are not states but for which statistical data are maintained on a separate and independent basis.

Preface

Many countries moved toward more flexible exchange rate regimes over the past decade, which reflects in part the belief that more flexible exchange rates provide a greater degree of monetary policy autonomy and flexibility in responding to external shocks, including large and volatile capital flows. There has often been a reluctance to let go of pegged exchange rates despite the benefits of flexible rates. The extensive institutional and operational requirements needed to support a floating exchange rate as well as difficulties in assessing the right time and manner to exit tend to be additional factors in this reluctance. This paper presents the concrete steps taken by certain countries in transitioning to greater exchange rate flexibility, with a view to elaborating on the operational ingredients that proved helpful in promoting successful and durable transitions. It attempts to provide a better understanding of how these various operational ingredients were established and coordinated with the exits, how their implementation interacted with macro and other conditions, and how they contributed to the smoothness of the exits.

The material in this paper was originally prepared in connection with a workshop on moving to greater exchange rate flexibility conducted in Ukraine in April 2005. The detailed case studies prepared subsequently also aimed at providing a follow-up to a discussion by the International Monetary Fund's (IMF) Executive Board in December 2004 on "From Fixed to Float: Operational Aspects of Moving Toward Exchange Rate Flexibility" (IMF, 2004b). In concluding the discussion, Directors asked for more guidance on the sequencing and order of importance of the operational elements, backed by analysis of more specific country experiences and cross-country studies.

The detailed country case studies and their syntheses were prepared by a team of experts under the guidance and direction of İnci Ötker-Robe, former Technical Assistance Wing, Europe, of the Monetary and Capital Markets Department (MCM). The experts, Luis Ahumada, Fernando Barrán, André Minella, Zbigniew Polański, Piotr Szpunar, Barry Topf, and David Vávra, are on the staff of the central banks of a number of countries that moved from various forms of pegged exchange rate regimes to floating exchange rates. The team collaborated closely with the former Exchange Regimes and Exchange Regime and Debt and Reserve Management Division (ER) of MCM, where the "Fixed to Float" paper (IMF, 2004a) had been prepared, in particular with Udaibir Das, Christian Mulder, and Eva Petrova. Neil Saker and Jahanara Zaman of ER contributed to two of the appendixes of this paper. Graham Colin-Jones provided editorial support and Maria Delia M. Araneta provided secretarial support. Sean Culhane of the External Relations Department edited the manuscript and coordinated the production of the publication.

The paper has benefited from comments of colleagues in MCM and in other departments of the IMF, and of Eduardo Loyo, Executive Director for Brazil. The views expressed in this paper are those of the IMF staff and do not necessarily reflect the views of national authorities or IMF Executive Directors.

Jaime Caruana

Director
Monetary and Capital Markets Department

Abbreviations

ACI	Financial Markets Association
BCU	Central Bank of Uruguay
BoI	Bank of Israel
CBB	Central Bank of Brazil
CBC	Central Bank of Chile
CFA	certified financial analyst
CNB	Czech National Bank
Copom	Monetary Policy Committee (Brazil)
CPI	consumer price index
EU	European Union
FX	foreign exchange
ISDA	International Swap Dealers Association
IT	inflation targeting
LTCM	Long-Term Capital Management
MPC	Monetary Policy Council (Poland)
NBP	National Bank of Poland
NBU	National Bank of Ukraine
NDF	nondeliverable forward
NIS	New Israel sheqel
OTC	over the counter
PPP	purchasing power parity
TA	technical assistance

Part 1
The Overall Framework and Synthesis of Country Experiences

I Overview

Many countries moved toward more flexible exchange rate regimes over the past decade.[1] Among the factors underlying the move to greater flexibility has been the belief that more flexible exchange rates provide a greater degree of monetary policy autonomy and flexibility in responding to external shocks, including large and volatile capital flows. Flexible exchange rates have been expected to (1) reduce one-way bets against currencies, thereby discouraging short-term capital inflows that can be easily reversed; (2) discourage a buildup of large unhedged foreign currency positions by reducing the implicit exchange rate guarantees implied by pegged and tightly managed exchange rates; and hence (3) stimulate prudent risk management and foreign exchange (FX) market development as market participants seek to hedge against potentially greater exchange rate risks.

There is often a reluctance to let go of pegged exchange rates despite these benefits (the so-called *fear of floating*). Policymakers tend to keep the pegs, reflecting, in general, the perceived costs of exchange rate volatility related to (1) concerns about losing policy credibility; (2) adverse effects of a potential appreciation of the domestic currency on external balances; (3) higher inflation from exchange rate pass-through (given the limited technical and institutional capacity to implement alternative monetary policy frameworks such as inflation targeting (IT), and underdeveloped financial markets characterized by larger exchange rate fluctuations); and (4) potential losses from currency mismatches, in particular when markets and instruments to hedge against risks are limited. The difficulties in assessing the right time to exit and in determining the alternative regime to adopt tend to be additional factors in this reluctance.

Such concerns about floating hence affect the pace and manner in which countries move to greater flex-

---

[1]See Eichengreen and others (1998), Fischer (2001), and literature cited therein.

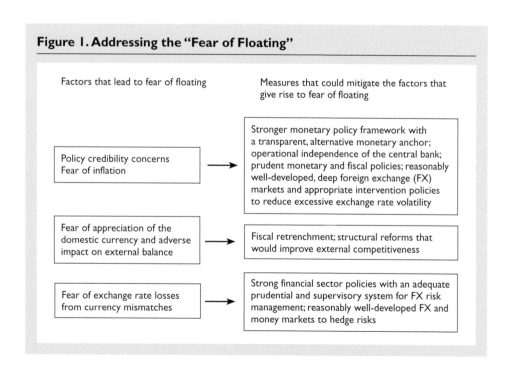

Figure 1. Addressing the "Fear of Floating"

Factors that lead to fear of floating

Measures that could mitigate the factors that give rise to fear of floating

Policy credibility concerns
Fear of inflation

→ Stronger monetary policy framework with a transparent, alternative monetary anchor; operational independence of the central bank; prudent monetary and fiscal policies; reasonably well-developed, deep foreign exchange (FX) markets and appropriate intervention policies to reduce excessive exchange rate volatility

Fear of appreciation of the domestic currency and adverse impact on external balance

→ Fiscal retrenchment; structural reforms that would improve external competitiveness

Fear of exchange rate losses from currency mismatches

→ Strong financial sector policies with an adequate prudential and supervisory system for FX risk management; reasonably well-developed FX and money markets to hedge risks

Box I. Fixed to Float: Operational Ingredients of Durable Exits to Flexible Exchange Rates

This box provides a brief summary of the main points of the IMF's operational framework for moving toward exchange rate flexibility.[1] This framework provides hands-on guidance on the institutional, operational, and technical aspects of moving toward exchange rate flexibility, presenting in turn a context for the country experiences in Part 1: Section II and Part 2.

Although the timing and priority accorded to each of these areas may vary from country to country depending on initial conditions and economic structure, the successful ingredients for floating include (1) developing a deep and liquid FX market, (2) formulating intervention policies consistent with the new exchange rate regime, (3) establishing an alternative nominal anchor in the context of a new monetary policy framework and developing supportive markets, and (4) reviewing exchange rate exposures and building the capacity of market participants to manage exchange rate risks and of the supervisory authorities to regulate and monitor them.[2]

Operating a flexible exchange rate regime works well only when there is a sufficiently liquid and efficient FX market for price discovery. A well-functioning FX market allows the exchange rate to respond to market forces, helps minimize disruptive day-to-day fluctuations in the exchange rate, and facilitates exchange rate

risk management. Developing (spot and forward) FX markets requires eliminating market-inhibiting regulations, improving the market microstructure (for example, by allowing risk-hedging instruments, simplifying FX legislation, or putting in place adequate payment and settlement systems), and increasing information flows in the market, while reducing the central bank's market-maker role. Allowing some exchange rate flexibility is a key step in limiting what is, to some extent, an unavoidable chicken-and-egg problem: Exchange rate flexibility requires a deep market and better risk management, but a deep market and prudent risk management require flexibility. Providing for a two-way risk is also important, in fostering better management of risks and minimizing destabilizing trading strategies (and, thereby, the risk of disorderly exits).

Private sector FX risk exposure can have an important bearing on the pace of the exit, the type of flexible exchange rate regime adopted, and intervention policies, requiring a careful management of the transfer of FX risk back to the private sector and systems to monitor and manage the private sector's exposures. In managing the FX risk, the market participants need to develop analytical and information systems to monitor and measure risks in addition to internal risk management and prudential procedures. Adequate prudential and supervisory arrangements and enforcement capacity also need to be in place so that banks' direct and indirect FX exposures and related risks can be monitored. Although early investment in these elements is typically beneficial by itself, it can also help mitigate the risk of disorderly exits; having an effective FX-risk-related supervisory and prudential framework can limit contagion of financial crises. Careful development of derivatives markets for foreign exchange with appropriate safeguards is an essential element in building capacity to manage FX risks, while limiting their potential misuse for speculative activity.

---

[1]Appendix I provides a more detailed summary, drawing on IMF (2004a and 2004b). The fixed-to-float framework was endorsed by the IMF's Executive Board in 2004, which reiterated that no single exchange rate regime is appropriate for all countries at all times (also see Eichengreen and others, 1998; and Mussa and others, 2000, on exchange rate issues).

[2]These are in addition to the role of sound macroeconomic and structural policies—including fiscal discipline, monetary policy credibility, and a sound financial sector—which are essential to maintaining any type of regime, fixed or floating.

ibility. Some countries that put significant emphasis on preparedness for floating chose a cautious and gradual approach to greater flexibility while working on establishing the necessary supportive elements of floating rates. In other countries, authorities experienced difficulty in managing the exits that occurred under market pressure when flexible exchange rates were adopted with little preparation devoted to addressing the fears of floating. Country experiences suggest that those that work on mitigating risks associated with floating (Figure 1) can achieve a smoother exit from their pegged regimes, even when the elements supporting greater flexibility are not fully in place before the move to greater flexibility.

An earlier IMF study described the institutional, operational, and technical aspects of moving toward flexibility that are important for a successful transition

(referred to henceforth as the fixed-to-float framework). The framework (provided in Duttagupta, Fernandez, and Karacadag, 2004, and subsequently endorsed by the IMF Executive Board in December 2004) concluded that for a successful transition to a floating regime, the following four "ingredients" were generally needed: (1) developing a deep and liquid FX market, (2) setting up adequate systems to review and manage exchange rate risks, (3) formulating coherent intervention policies consistent with the new regime, and (4) establishing an appropriate alternative nominal anchor in the context of the new monetary policy framework (IMF, 2004a and 2004b). This framework is summarized in Box 1.

This paper presents the concrete steps a selected number of countries took in transitioning to greater exchange rate flexibility, elaborating on the operational

Figure 2b. Exchange Rate Regime Evolutions: Fast Disorderly Exits

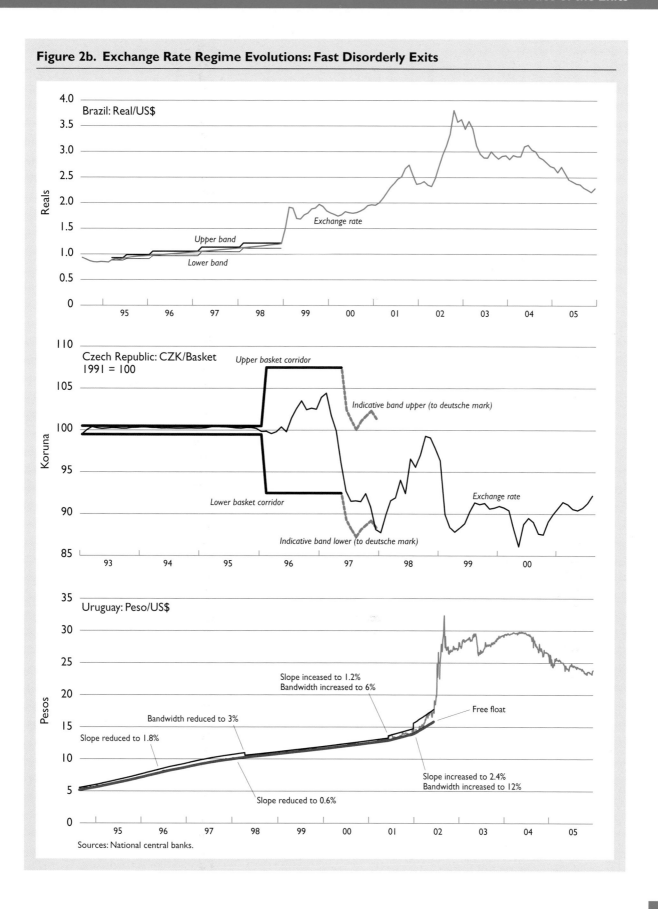

Sources: National central banks.

Table 2. Country Experiences with Transition from Pegged to Flexible Regimes: Motivation and Triggers of Exit

	Brazil	Chile	Czech Republic	Israel	Poland	Uruguay
Shifting long-term monetary policy objectives	In both regimes, the main concern was to keep inflation at low levels and avoid return of high inflation.	Increasing inconsistency between competitiveness and inflation objectives was a prime motivation.	Not a major role in the exit, although disinflation did not proceed and monetary targets were missed.	Greater exchange rate flexibility introduced as a part of the move toward inflation targeting (IT).	Changing policy objectives (stabilization, competitiveness, disinflation) were important in phasing the exit. The need for disinflation affected the move from a crawling band to float and adopting IT.	Not a major factor in the exit. In fact, the authorities deliberately kept the exchange rate at the strong (lower) limit of the crawling band (avoiding exchange rate volatility) prior to the exit as a means to disinflate the economy. Absence of monetary anchor after the exit (foreign exchange (FX) and banking crisis) led to preparations for adopting IT.
Deteriorating macroeconomic/financial fundamentals undermining the sustainability of the peg	Increasing current account deficits and public debt; loose fiscal policy; high domestic interest rates.	Exchange rate pass-through declining since mid-1990s; competitiveness concerns affected band parameters before float; implicit IT regime and balanced fiscal policy helped build monetary policy credibility.	Overheating economy with rising inflation; exchange rate pass-through high; large current account (CA) deficit; real/nominal appreciation; monetary tightening triggered by expansionary fiscal policy incompatible with the peg.	Competitiveness pressures played some role in introducing more flexibility early on and in periodic devaluations of the central parity.	Competitiveness concerns affected monetary policy conduct until late 1990s, and played a role in moving to a crawling peg in the early 1990s.	Banking crisis (foreign currency-denominated deposits fell by more than 40 percent), leading to a large fall of international reserves.
Ability to respond to external shocks, including increased capital inflows	Noncrisis periods: capital inflows leading to sterilization operations. Crises: use of international reserves and sharp increases in interest rates.	Complications arising from increased capital flows in the process of integration into financial markets.	Massive sterilization to limit impact of capital inflows, not very successfully, though the ability to sterilize seemed relatively high.	Capacity to respond to external shocks an important element in introducing the bands. Problems in sterilizing capital flows led to adoption of crawling fan.	Inflows of FX from CA surpluses and capital inflows played a role in introducing more FX flexibility by adopting a crawling band.	Not a major factor. The monetary policy regime with exchange rate targeting had not experienced serious difficulties in dealing with capital inflows prior to the exit.
Contagion from international financial market turbulences	External crises put significant pressure on the exchange rate system. Russian crisis accelerated the collapse of the regime.	Fears of contagion from the Asian and Russian crises had delayed the elimination of the band.	Short-term capital flight following the Asian crisis was the immediate trigger of the exit crisis.	Not important.	Not very important.	Sudden stop and capital outflow following Argentina crisis key in floating. Before, the band was widened in response to Argentina's float.
Desire to increase the perception of FX risk	Not a main factor.	Some effect on pace of move to flexibility; fear of balance sheet effects on corporates contributed to delay in exit in the 1990s.	Played a role in introducing a buy/sell spread for fixing transaction with the Czech National Bank (CNB) and widening of the band before the exit.	Introducing a basket of currencies and widening the crawling band through a fan system was partly motivated by the desire to encourage risk management.	Some effect on the pace of introducing more flexibility because concerns arose that the corporate sector could not cope with fast appreciation.	Not a main factor.

Source: Detailed case studies.

of establishing credibility. Nevertheless, the existence of some of the supporting factors (see below) helped limit the period of instability after the float (Brazil and Czech Republic).

Factors that Triggered the Move to Greater Flexibility

Greater flexibility was introduced in general when multiple monetary policy objectives became increasingly more incompatible (Table 2). A growing emphasis on reducing inflation as compared with other goals (for example, competitiveness) was the main incentive for the gradual exits. At the initial stages of the transition, a desire to strike a balance between the goals of reducing inflation and safeguarding competitiveness led in general to the adoption of preannounced crawling pegs. The need for greater flexibility grew as countries opened capital accounts and received inflows that complicated monetary management: Efforts to maintain inflation and exchange rate targets simultaneously required large-scale sterilizations that eventually became costly or even counterproductive by stimulating further inflows. Flexible exchange rates helped absorb the impact of the inflows and let the authorities set interest rates at levels consistent with inflation targets. Reduced implicit exchange rate guarantees helped limit incentives for speculative inflows.

The forced exits were triggered by contagion from international financial crises that revealed the countries' domestic macroeconomic or financial vulnerabilities and policy inconsistencies. All three countries experienced downward pressure on their currencies from the ongoing market turbulence in other emerging markets (the Russian crisis for Brazil, the Asian crisis for the Czech Republic, and the Argentine crisis for Uruguay), which led to an eventual collapse of the pegged regimes. Tight domestic monetary policies had attracted significant short-term capital inflows, with those inflows leading to, in the context of exchange-rate-based stabilizations and absence of fiscal policy support, rising external deficits and overheating pressures; the overheating pressures in turn put pressure on the sustainability of the pegs (Brazil and Czech Republic). In Uruguay, financial vulnerabilities in the highly dollarized public and private sectors, when combined with external shocks that amplified the external imbalances, undermined market confidence and played a role in the collapse of the crawling band.

In some cases, desire to encourage better risk management provided an additional motivation for moving to greater flexibility. In Israel, for example, the move to a crawling fan regime in mid-1997 was aimed at increasing the perception of two-way risk in the exchange rate:

By allowing an asymmetric widening of the crawling band on the weaker limit of the band, the authorities raised the potential scope for depreciation, while in fact the stronger (more appreciated) limit of the band was under pressure. This regime shift, combined with the nonintervention policy of the Bank of Israel (BoI), in effect helped the private sector realize that it had to cope with FX uncertainty, which encouraged, in turn, the development of FX hedging tools. In other words, greater exchange rate flexibility provided a means for mitigating some of the risks associated with flexible exchange rates, thereby reinforcing itself.

Coordination of Transitions with the Supporting Elements of a Floating Regime

Country experiences summarized below support the fixed-to-float framework by showing that advance preparation pays off in attaining a smooth and durable transition to flexible regimes. Having the main ingredients of flexibility fully in place before the switch to a full float (Table 3) provided a coherent transition process and contributed to the orderly nature of the exits in the gradually exiting countries. In particular, agreement on the principles of the transition process and characteristics of the regime to be exited helped provide a framework for the process. Establishing the individual supporting elements was also mutually reinforcing, in that introducing some flexibility allowed some capacity building for floating, which in turn permitted more exchange rate flexibility. Advance preparation was crucial in avoiding costly crisis exits from pegs, as well as in moderating the severity of exits under market pressure.

The importance of the appropriate degree of preparedness is also underscored by the experiences of those countries that either reversed or experienced delays in their transition to greater flexibility. The experiences of those that reversed their initial decision to move to greater flexibility point to a number of operational weaknesses (Appendix II), including an underdeveloped and illiquid foreign exchange market (Uzbekistan), a limited capacity to manage exchange rate risk (Ecuador, Uzbekistan, and Pakistan), a lack of appropriate intervention policy (Uzbekistan and Pakistan), and a limited institutional and technical capacity to adopt a credible alternative nominal anchor (Uzbekistan and Pakistan). Likewise, Ukraine's ongoing experience with moving to a flexible regime underscores the importance of quickly establishing the necessary ingredients of a floating regime (Appendix III); intensive efforts to do so could limit the risks of policy reversals and help ensure that the absence of the essential ingredients does not slow the transition process.

Table 3. Extent of Preparedness for Transitioning to Greater Flexibility: Before the Full Float[1]

	Orderly Exits			Exits under Pressure		
	Chile (1984–99)	Israel (1985–2005)	Poland (1990–2000)	Brazil (1999)	Czech Rep. (1996–97)	Uruguay (2002)
Ingredients of a Floating Regime						
(1) FX market development						
Spot markets	√	√	√	√	√	√
Derivative markets/hedging instruments	√	√	√[2]	√ (futures)	√[2]	X
Complementary markets						
Interbank money market	√	√[3]	√	√	√	√[4]
Securities market	√	√[3]	√	√	√	√[4]
(2) FX risk management capacity	√	√	√	X[5]	√	X
(3) Alternative monetary policy framework	√	√	√	X	X	X
Monetary policy implementation capacity	√	√	√	√	√	X
(4) Intervention strategy for a floating regime	With the float	√	With the float	With the float	√	With the float
Overall preparedness	Well prepared	Well prepared	Well prepared	Reasonably well prepared	Reasonably well prepared	Not well prepared
Memo: Capital Account Liberalization						
Short-term capital inflows liberalized	√[6]	√	√[7]	√[6]	√[7]	√
Capital outflows liberalized	√[6]	√	√[7]	√	√[7]	√
Derivative transactions liberalized	√	√	√[7]	√	√[7]	√

Source: Detailed case studies.

Note: FX = foreign exchange.

[1]The years in parentheses refer to the period of transition to a full float.

[2]Major boom one year before the float.

[3]Lagged behind compared to the foreign exchange markets.

[4]For maturities less than 270 days.

[5]The prudential framework was not in place to control the overall risk exposure of banks, with identified shortcomings mainly regarding the prudential regulation of banks' exposure to FX risk. Corporates in general (and banks) were making active use of the futures markets to hedge their exposures or to take speculative positions. Market participants were not accustomed to assessing, as a matter of routine, the FX risks posed by regular market volatility.

[6]For Chile, all controls were removed shortly before or with the float. For Brazil, controls were liberalized gradually during the 1990s (inflow controls of 1993–96 liberalized by 1999), with further liberalization for nonresident investments after the float.

[7]In the Czech Republic, most inflows and outflows had been liberalized by 1997, but certain inflow transactions (including financial derivatives) were liberalized in early 1999, following a transition period to phase out the remaining controls under the agreement with the Organization for Economic Cooperation and Development (OECD), with full liberalization taking place in 2002. Similarly in Poland, full liberalization of all capital account transactions took place in 2002, until which time certain transactions (including selective derivatives operations and short-term portfolio and deposit transactions) had remained controlled.

A Deep and Liquid FX Market

In the case of gradual exits, the FX market was illiquid and undeveloped at the beginning of the transition process, often dominated by the central bank as the sole market maker. The central bank's role through its fixing mechanism was gradually reduced as markets developed; fixing formally ended in Israel in 1990 and Poland in 1999. In most cases, market development began only after some exchange rate flexibility was introduced: in Israel, when the exchange rate was allowed to vary within a ±5 percent band; in Chile, after widening of the band to ±5 percent; and in Poland,

following the adoption of a crawling band with a ±7.0 percent width. In the Czech Republic, too, where some flexibility had been introduced in 1996 shortly before the disorderly exit, the market developed more rapidly after the band was widened from ±0.5 percent to ±7.5 percent. In most cases, the market mechanism began as a direct interbank market (in Israel, it began with an intermediate stage of a multilateral auction in 1990–94 when a continuous interbank market was introduced).

In all cases, the spot FX market was the first to develop, followed by derivatives (forward, swap, options, and futures) markets (Table 4 and Figures 3 and 4). The spot markets had been well developed in all six

Exchange rate regime

Basket Peg | Horizontal Band | Crawling Band | Crawling Fan (de facto float) | Free Float

IT capacity

FX market

Capital inflow liberalization

Monetary policy operational capacity

- CB bills introduced
- Interest rate targeting
- Full corridor system introduced

FX risk management and regulation

- Annual inflation targets
- Multi-year inflation targets
- Full-fledged IT
- Basel I requirements introduced
- Limits on FX open positions
- Requirement to adopt policies to manage direct/indirect FX exposures by 1997
- Stricter reporting and assessment of indirect FX risk/exposure
- Reporting on FX risk policies, capital charges for FX risk
- Higher reserve provisions against FX risk/exposure

- CB market maker
- CB sells FX options
- Fixing ends, Multi-lateral auctions
- OTC market for FX options
- Continuous interbank market; exchange-traded FX options
- First interbank broker
- Options to euro introduced

Intervention policies

- CB fixing
- Smoothing operations inside the band
- Inner band
- Reduction of interventions, soon resumed
- Interventions stopped (formal policy of no intervention)

Capital outflow liberalization

- Long-term inflows liberalized
- Short-term inflows liberalize
- Futures transactions of residents permitted
- Financial investment liberalized
- FDI liberalized
- Most other outflows liberalized
- All restrictions on nonresidents lifted
- Full liberalization
- Full liberalization

1987 1988 1989 1990 1991 1992 1993 1994 1995 1996 1997 1998 1999 2000 2001 2002 2003 2004 2005 2006

Israel

Figure 3 (concluded)

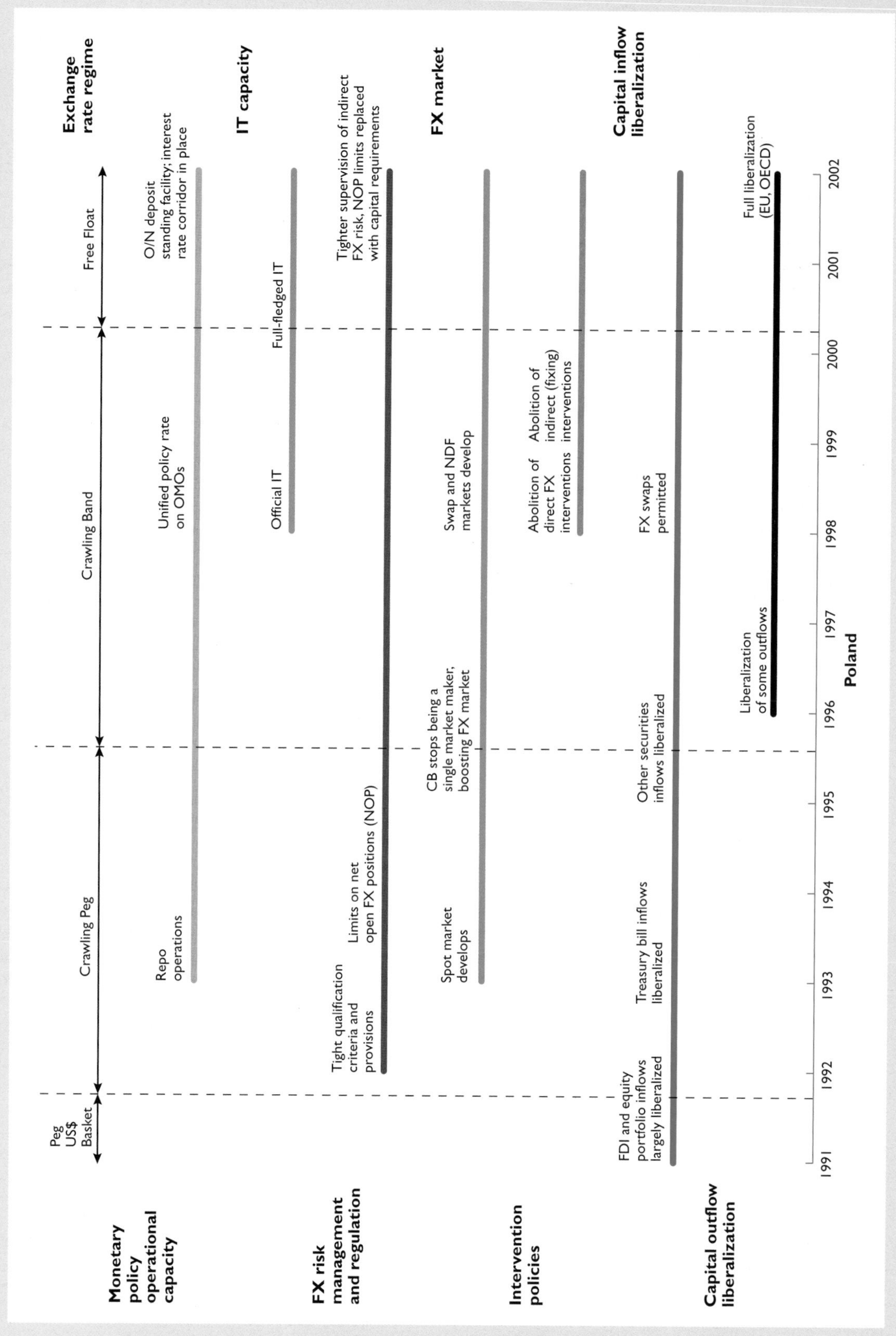

Poland

When liberalizing derivative transactions, the authorities established some precautions to limit such risks (for example, documentation requirements to prove the legitimacy of the underlying transactions so as to limit speculative activity, and prudential and supervisory rules to mitigate excessive risk taking linked with the use of derivatives). In Chile, FX operations and derivatives transactions were initially permitted only to support trade activities or investments abroad. The authorization requirement to engage in derivatives transactions with external counterparties was eliminated at the time of the float. In Israel, documentation requirements were used for underlying transactions for a considerable period. Forward transactions were permitted in stages by tenor (for example, first forwards up to one month, then three months, then six months, and then one year, at which point all restrictions were lifted). Although the use of options was not considered an avenue for speculation and options market development was promoted actively, documentation requirements were maintained to indicate that options were used for hedging purposes. Banks' direct and indirect exposures to FX risks associated with derivative transactions were also incorporated in prudential systems (for example, forward exposures in open FX positions and in capital requirements (Israel, Poland)).

Systems to Assess and Manage FX Risks

In most countries studied, the private sector had a reasonable capacity to manage FX risk exposure at the time of the float (Table 4). This capacity developed along with a strengthening of the prudential and supervisory framework in the Czech Republic and Poland, though without specific consideration for FX risks (except for limits on open positions); explicit incorporation of indirect FX risks (for example, in capital or loan classification requirements) came only after the float in the context of harmonizing prudential systems according to European Union directives. In Chile and Israel, building the FX risk management capacity went hand in hand with an explicit recognition, regulation, and reporting of banks' FX exposures.[7] In all four countries, it was also supported by a gradual liberalization of swap and forward transactions throughout the transition process, which facilitated hedging. In the Czech Republic, the ability to manage FX risks in turn assisted the transition to

flexibility and limited a potential spillover of currency pressures into a financial crisis.

Commercial banks' capacity to manage FX risks was also supported by the gradual increase in exchange rate flexibility and discontinuation of central bank intervention within the crawling bands. In all four countries, reduced implicit exchange rate guarantees implied by greater flexibility stimulated risk recognition of market participants, enabled them to learn early on to work with exchange risks, and contributed to the development of derivative instruments to hedge such risks. In Chile, for example, greater room for exchange rate changes within a widening band encouraged hedging onshore or offshore. The currency mismatches in the banking and corporate sectors were limited, and about 90 to 100 percent of bank and 40 percent of corporate exposures were hedged. In Israel, the nonintervention policy of the BoI from mid-1997 made FX risks explicit, and responsibility to manage the risk was imposed on those incurring the risk (banks and nonfinancial businesses); this in turn led to a fall in net FX liabilities and stimulated the growth of hedging instruments.

In Brazil and Uruguay, there was room for improvement in FX risk management at the time of the exit. In Uruguay, the supervisory and regulatory environment, although being strengthened to increase banks' resilience, had not specifically addressed the rising FX risk in a highly dollarized economy. FX-related prudential rules were tightened after a major bank restructuring following the float.[8] In Brazil, there were no limits on global FX risk exposures of financial institutions in terms of capital, but there were more direct restrictions that would affect FX activity.[9] Nevertheless, the private sector's unhedged FX risk exposure was rather limited through natural hedging, issuance of dollar-indexed public debt, and derivatives transactions. Specific regulations were put in place after the float, and banks were asked to use stress testing for such risks. Although building this capacity during a crisis was difficult, efforts in this direction helped boost market confidence while also reducing the risk of future problems and potential costs of exchange rate fluctuations under flexible rates.

The experiences suggest that a relatively stable financial system with little FX exposure was important in achieving a smooth exit. In Brazil and the Czech Republic, banks had no significant FX exposure, which likely helped limit contagion from the currency crises

---

[7]The regulation and reporting of FX risks included, for example, net open FX position limits (in Chile and Israel); inclusion of debtors' currency mismatches in assessing repayment capacity and minimum credit rating requirements for external borrowing by corporations (in Chile); and the requirement to incorporate FX exposures in capital and reporting requirements and FX credits in provisioning requirements, use of stress tests for indirect FX exposures, reporting of FX risk management policies by banks, and maintenance of FX liquidity requirements (in Israel).

[8]Liquidity requirements on FX deposits were raised, unhedged FX risks were incorporated in loan classification and provisioning requirements, and currency-specific capital requirements were imposed.

[9]There were restrictions on foreign currency positions in bank balance sheets: No bank deposits in foreign currency were allowed, and external loans were on-lent with obligatory dollar-indexed clauses to avoid currency mismatch problems. There were also specific limits on long positions and a limit on short positions contingent on banks' adjusted net worth, both in the spot market.

Figure 4. Sequencing of Transitions with Supporting Elements: Fast Disorderly Exits

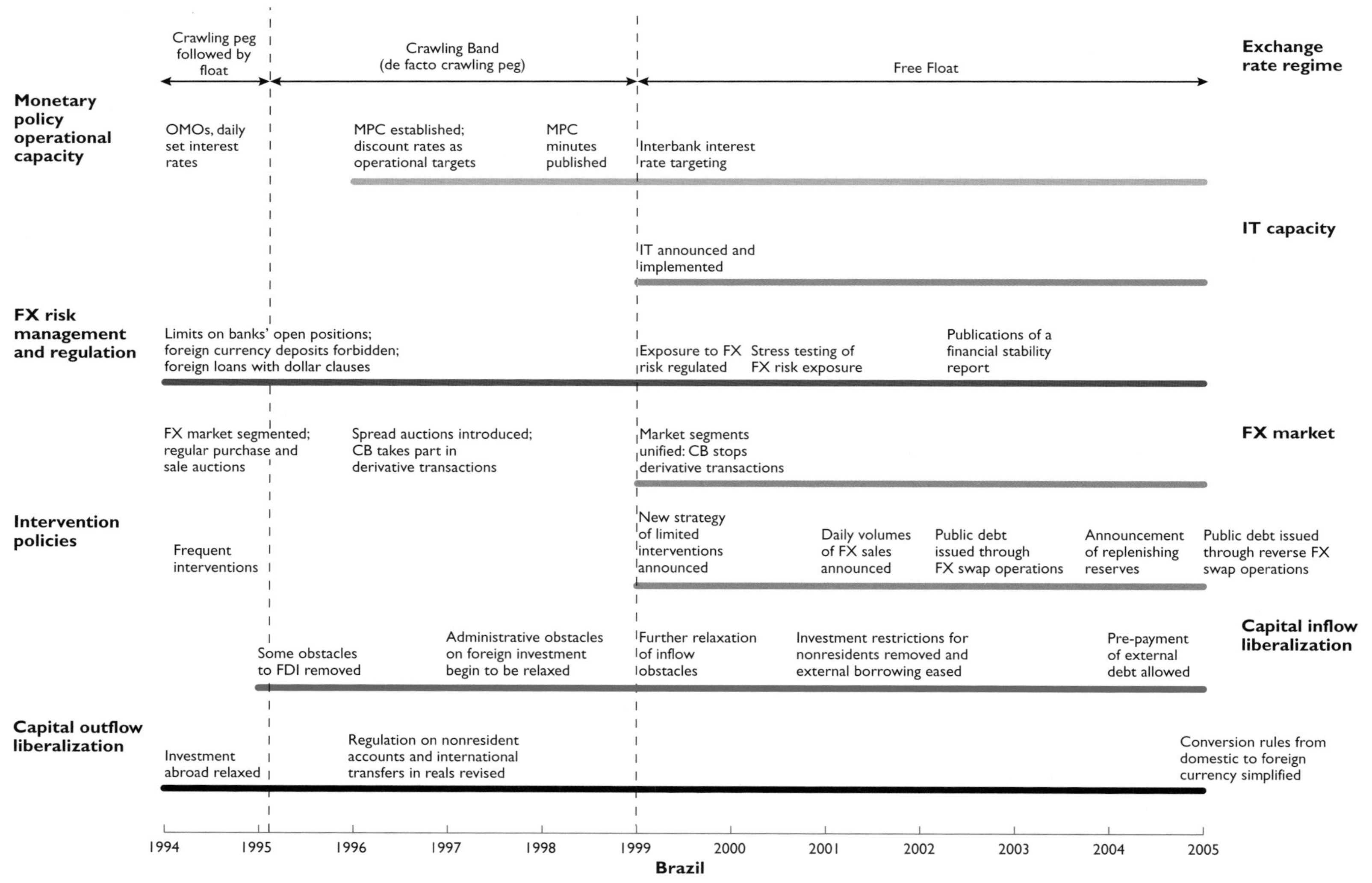

Brazil

Timeline: 1994 1995 1996 1997 1998 1999 2000 2001 2002 2003 2004 2005

Exchange rate regime

- Crawling peg followed by float
- Crawling Band (de facto crawling peg)
- Free Float

Monetary policy operational capacity

- OMOs, daily set interest rates
- MPC established; discount rates as operational targets
- MPC minutes published
- Interbank interest rate targeting

IT capacity

- IT announced and implemented

FX risk management and regulation

- Limits on banks' open positions; foreign currency deposits forbidden; foreign loans with dollar clauses
- Exposure to FX risk regulated
- Stress testing of FX risk exposure
- Publications of a financial stability report

FX market

- FX market segmented; regular purchase and sale auctions
- Spread auctions introduced; CB takes part in derivative transactions
- Market segments unified: CB stops derivative transactions

Intervention policies

- Frequent interventions
- New strategy of limited interventions announced
- Daily volumes of FX sales announced
- Public debt issued through FX swap operations
- Announcement of replenishing reserves
- Public debt issued through reverse FX swap operations

Capital inflow liberalization

- Some obstacles to FDI removed
- Administrative obstacles on foreign investment begin to be relaxed
- Further relaxation of inflow obstacles
- Investment restrictions for nonresidents removed and external borrowing eased
- Pre-payment of external debt allowed

Capital outflow liberalization

- Investment abroad relaxed
- Regulation on nonresident accounts and international transfers in reals revised
- Conversion rules from domestic to foreign currency simplified

internal instability and reducing the speed of currency depreciation. The CBC also announced that it would inform the market about such decisions. No explicit predetermined rule for intervention was established, but explicit communication of intervention intensity was considered important for credibility. So that they do not become a common practice, interventions have been made transparent and details announced in advance, including the specific period during which the CBC could intervene and the maximum amounts to be used. Interventions were aimed at providing a signal to the market that the authorities considered the evolution of the exchange rate not justified by fundamentals and the extent of the depreciation excessive (De Gregorio and Tokman, 2004).[6]

Sequencing with Capital Account Liberalization

Chile's capital account liberalization gradually moved parallel to its exchange rate liberalization (Le Fort-Varela, 2005). The adjustments in the regulations aimed to support the crawling band by reducing the net inflow of capital and stemming the appreciation of the peso. Following the surge in capital inflows, capital outflows were gradually liberalized along with the widening of the band.[7] In addition, controls were imposed on short-term capital inflows from June 1991, aimed at retaining the possibility of managing the exchange rate with an independent monetary policy. These controls were primarily market based, in the form of an unremunerated reserve requirement, and were tightened several times to increase the rate or to broaden its scope (see Ariyoshi and others, 2000; and Le Fort-Varela, 2005). The inflow controls were lifted in 1998, and all remaining controls on inflows and outflows were removed in 2001, well after the regime shift. Controls on derivatives transactions were relaxed from the mid-1990s to 1999 to facilitate the handling of FX risks under more flexible exchange rates.

Other Supporting Elements

At the time of the move to a floating regime, the banking sector was sound and compliant with supervision and regulation. The banking sector, built over the 1990s, had a sustained large capital base and kept a low level of dollarization, accompanied by a strict regulatory and supervisory framework that limited banks' exposure to credit and currency risks. Chile also successfully created a unit of indexation to hedge inflation risk. Since the early 1980s this unit has been widely used in deposit contracts and to finance long-run real estate loans. The quality of the loan portfolio of the banks was high, with nonperforming loans reaching at most 3 percent of total loans under the worst-case scenarios before the Asian crisis.[8]

A well-developed domestic capital market also supported the flexible exchange rate regime. The development of the domestic capital market allowed several firms to change the composition of their debt by issuing long-term bonds denominated in Chilean pesos to reduce their FX exposures and vulnerability to large depreciations in the currency. The development of the capital market was due in part to the increasing importance of institutional investors, mainly pension funds, which made up a sizable share of the demand for debt instruments in the domestic market through the 1990s.

A prudent fiscal policy was also a key ingredient in Chile's success in disinflation and transition to a new nominal anchor (Morandé, 2001). Over this period, fiscal authorities managed to maintain a fiscal surplus, which allowed monetary authorities to implement a monetary policy that eventually lowered inflation from two-digit chronic levels to those observed in developed countries.

Challenges Faced and Lessons from Chile's Transition Experience

Chile's transition to a full float was a fairly lengthy process because of the significant emphasis the authorities placed on the presence of the supportive elements for a floating regime. The regime shift took about 15 years, even though the economy was apparently well prepared, with the essential conditions already in place well before the float. The trigger for the eventual decision seems to have been the extent to which the prevailing multiple monetary objectives became incompatible. As in the other gradually exiting countries (Israel and Poland), the monetary authorities considered that it would be hard to defend an exchange rate band that allowed for a gradual depreciation of the currency within a crawling band, while at the same time ful-

---

[6]The CBC has intervened in the market twice since 1999: first in August 2001, in response to the regional financial disorder caused by the crisis in Argentina, followed by the turbulence in international capital markets after the events of September 11. The CBC announced that from that date to the end of the year, it could intervene in the FX market that was operating under a free floating regime; it also announced the resources available for intervention. The second intervention took place in October 2002 and was attributed to the pressures on the Brazilian real. Both attempts to influence the exchange rate are considered to have been successful. Similar announcements were made in October 2003 for possible FX intervention (Tapia and Tokman, 2004).

[7]The minimum time to repatriate capital and earnings for FDI capital was reduced successively during 1991–93 from 10 years in 1985 to 1 year in 1993, and eliminated in 2000. Banks were allowed to invest abroad up to 40 percent of their funds collected as term deposits in 1991, and the amounts that pension funds were allowed to invest abroad were increased successively during 1992–99.

[8]The Basel I framework was incorporated only in 1997 along with a substantial amendment of the banking law, which broadened the scope of banking activities.

filling the inflation rate target. The pace of the exit, however, seems to have been greatly affected by the authorities' comfort level about the preparedness of the economy.

The main challenge confronting the authorities was to determine whether the economy was sufficiently prepared for the floating regime. Assessing the state of preparedness for the float and hence the right time to move was difficult. In particular, the authorities had feared that the liberalization of the exchange rate and the associated volatility in the FX market could endanger the low and stable inflation goal and, therefore, the credibility of the central bank, as well as the financial stability of the economy.[9] In fact, the fear of losses from currency mismatches in the corporate sector and of the potential pass-through of exchange rate changes to inflation contributed to delaying the exit by several years.

The lack of reliable and prompt information to assess these risks was the main contributor to the difficulty of assessing the level of preparedness. The degree of exchange rate pass-though, which the authorities had considered to be high, was actually decreasing over the 1990s, and hence was overestimated, especially in light of the consumer price index (CPI) inflation index.[10] Similarly, the lack of reliable, prompt information about the balance sheets of the corporate and household sectors and uncertainty about the level of development of the domestic derivatives market undermined the authorities' ability to assess the potential negative consequences of a sudden exchange rate depreciation. The mismatches turned out to be less substantial and the availability of hedging better than had been assumed. The widespread use of dollar-peso forward operations introduced in 1992 and the deep market for peso-indexed bonds allowed market participants to hedge against currency risk.

The following lessons can be drawn from Chile's experience with the regime transition:

- The gradual evolution of exchange rate flexibility and capital account liberalization can support each other. A gradual increase in the flexibility of the exchange rate helped Chile obtain the benefits of a growing integration with capital markets, while lessening its risks. Gradual liberalization of capital outflows, a more cautious liberalization of the

short-term inflows, and an early liberalization of derivative transactions facilitated this integration, as market participants gained expertise and monetary authorities prepared for a move to a full float.

- Early preparation helps address fears of floating and increases the chances of a successful and smooth exit. In the case of Chile, building the capacity to manage FX risks and implement monetary operations, developing FX markets, and preparing since the early 1990s for an alternative monetary anchor toward full-fledged IT were vital in making a smooth transition to a floating regime. In addition, the CBC's transparent and effectively communicated intervention strategy also contributed to establishing the credibility of the floating regime and the IT framework.

- The availability of a timely and adequate information base is crucial in assessing the extent of preparedness. In the case of Chile, prompt information on private sector balance sheets and on dynamics between the exchange rate and inflation could have helped avoid an undue delay in moving to greater flexibility, which in turn could have been helpful in responding to external shocks that hit the domestic economy in the late 1990s.

- The Chilean experience also illustrates the mutually reinforcing relationship between greater exchange rate flexibility and market and capacity building: Introducing greater flexibility through a gradually widening crawling band encouraged better FX risk management and spot and forward FX market development, which in turn helped support the move to a fully flexible exchange rate regime in 1999.

- Finally, building a sound financial system and a deep capital market is also crucial in avoiding potentially disruptive consequences of a move to a flexible exchange rate regime. The strict supervision and regulation of the banking system, the emergence of a large institutional investor base, and the successful introduction of various financial instruments (for example, inflation-indexed bonds) were helpful in coping with greater exchange rate volatility under the floating regime.

Israel (1985–2005)[11]

Israel's transition from a pegged exchange rate to a floating exchange rate was extremely gradual, lasting

---

[9]After many years of intervention in the FX market and a relatively predictable nominal exchange rate, the corporate sector could have developed significant exposure to FX risk and greater exchange rate volatility.

[10]The diminishing pass-through over the CPI could have also been the consequence of the institutional credibility gained by the central bank and the government in successfully pursuing lower inflation and a sustained policy of a balanced budget. Hence, depreciations of the exchange rate could be perceived by agents as a transitory adjustment mechanism to changes in external conditions.

---

[11]Prepared by Barry Topf (Bank of Israel). The author thanks Sarah Cohen for her assistance with data, and numerous staff of the BoI for the information and experience they provided.

exactly 20 years, from 1985 until 2005. In fact, gradualism was a central principle of monetary policy, with a clear preference for moving in small incremental steps, which in aggregate and over time produced the desired results. The exchange rate regime evolved continuously in response to changing economic conditions and to the need to resolve conflicts emerging from the pursuit of multiple objectives in an increasingly global environment. Although there was no deliberate overall plan at the beginning of the transition, the process was coherent, based on gradual steps that strengthened credibility while avoiding reversals, integration with supporting measures in other areas, and prompt and appropriate responses to emerging concerns before they could lead to severe pressures.

Factors Motivating the Transition

Israel's transition from a fixed peg—the nominal anchor in a heterodox disinflation plan—to increasing exchange rate flexibility was part of the move to an IT regime. Over 20 years, Israel moved from a monetary policy based on exchange rate targeting to one based on IT. Policy over that period was aimed at resolving the conflicts that arose from trying to achieve multiple and sometimes conflicting objectives. Details of the changes in the exchange rate regime and its parameters are presented in Table 7.

From Fixed Peg to the U.S. Dollar to a Basket Peg

The fixed peg to the U.S. dollar adopted as part of the Economic Stabilization Plan of 1985 helped stabilize the economy, but its limitations quickly became apparent. The single currency peg was meant to quickly restore nominal stability and achieve credibility in anti-inflationary policies, given the widespread direct and indirect impact of the exchange rate on the Israeli economy. Inflation fell immediately from 400 percent to 20 percent per annum, in part because of the visibility of exchange rates and their impact on expectations. Although the peg was advantageous in terms of transparency and public perception, it did result in exposure to changes in the international value of the dollar during a period when cross rates were especially volatile. In an effort to reduce this exposure, after one year the sheqel was pegged to a basket of currencies that reflected the composition of Israel's international trade.

In addition to reducing the impact of fluctuations in world exchange rates, the peg to a basket rather than a single currency brought additional benefits. It introduced an element of flexibility by allowing variation in the bilateral exchange rates (especially against the dollar) most visible to the public and encouraged more sophisticated risk management as market participants understood the need to hedge against changes in the basket. The composition of the currency basket was reviewed annually and changed, if deemed necessary, according to predetermined rules, without affecting the exchange rate prevailing at the time.

From Basket Peg to Horizontal Band

Although fixed exchange rates contributed to restoring credibility to economic policy and reducing inflation, their drawbacks became more apparent over time. With inflation higher in Israel than among its trading partners, the sheqel underwent considerable real appreciation and loss of competitiveness. The unsustainability of fixed exchange rates, given large and persistent inflation differentials, made the sheqel the target of speculative attacks, which led to periodic devaluations. In addition, the lack of flexibility in exchange rates led to a lack of balance in policy tools: All adjustments (for example, to external shocks) had to be made solely through changes in interest rates or foreign currency reserves, which led to wide swings in both. The desire to avoid such swings led to the adoption of horizontal bands in January 1989.

Horizontal bands introduced an element of flexibility in exchange rates while reducing volatility and maintaining confidence in the disinflationary process still under way. The exchange rate—in basket terms—could vary within predetermined limits around an announced central rate. The exchange rate against any single currency, including the dollar, was a function of international cross rates. The horizontal band system led to a significant decrease in the volatility of interest rates and more stability in the level of foreign currency reserves. However, the still-large inflation differentials between Israel and its trading partners, together with the discrete nature of changes in the central rate, continued to induce large capital movements and speculative pressure on the sheqel. As a result, the central rate was devalued four times in three years, by amounts ranging from 6 to 10 percent.

The width of the band was initially set at ±3 percent, and widened to ±5 percent after approximately one year. A ±3 percent width was established to balance the need for sufficient flexibility to give substance to the band while avoiding excessive volatility in the exchange rate, which was still an important nominal anchor. Any narrower band was perceived as providing neither sufficient impetus for market development nor sufficient flexibility to relieve some of the strain on interest rates and FX reserves. On the other hand, moving too quickly to too wide a band might have introduced excessive volatility into the system without adequate time to adjust by, for example, introducing more sophisticated risk management practices. Once the market had adjusted smoothly to the ±3 percent band, widening it to ±5 percent was continuation of the policy of allowing greater flexibility.

Table 7. Evolution of Israel's Exchange Rate Regimes, 1985–2005

Date of Change	Regime	Event
July 1, 1985	Peg to dollar	New Israeli sheqel (NIS) devalued by 18.8%[1] and fixed at US$1.5
August 1, 1986	Peg to currency basket	NIS fixed at 1.49 to basket[2]
January 13, 1987		NIS devalued by 10% to 1.68
December 27, 1988		NIS devalued by 5% to 1.80
January 3, 1989	Horizontal band	Midpoint established at 1.95 (devaluation of 8%); limits established at ±3%
June 23, 1989		Midpoint raised by 6% to 2.06
March 1, 1990		Midpoint raised by 6% to 2.19; band widened to ±5%
September 10, 1990		Midpoint raised by 10% to 2.41
March 11, 1991		Midpoint raised by 6% to 2.55
December 17, 1991	Crawling band	Midpoint raised by 3% to 2.62; slope set at 9%
November 9, 1992		Midpoint raised by 3% to 2.93; slope reduced to 8%
July 26, 1993		Midpoint raised by 2% to 3.15; slope reduced to 6%
May 31, 1995		Midpoint raised by 0.8% to 3.53; band widened to ±7%; no change to slope
June 18, 1997	Crawling fan	Band widened to approximately ±14%[3]
		Slope of lower (strong) limit set at 4%
		Slope of upper limit set at 6%
August 17, 1998		Slope of lower limit set at 2%
		Slope of upper limit remains 6%
December 24, 2001		Strong limit lowered by 1% and fixed at constant 4.10 (slope set at 0)
		Slope of upper limit remains 6%
June 9, 2005	Free float	Band abolished

Source: Bank of Israel.

[1]Exchange rates and percentage changes approximate.

[2]From 1986, all exchanges rates in currency basket terms. The composition of the basket was US$ (60 percent), sterling (10 percent), yen (5 percent), deutsche mark (20 percent), and French franc (5 percent) in 1986; in 2004, the weights were 60 percent (US$), 5.9 percent (sterling), 5.6 percent (yen), 23.9 percent (euro).

[3]From June 18, 1997, exchange rate policy related only to the limits of the exchange rate band, and not to the midpoint, which was then used for statistical purposes only.

From Horizontal to Crawling Bands

In December 1991, the crawling band replaced the horizontal band; this change was made primarily to prevent periodic speculative cycles around realignments of the central rate. In the crawling band regime, the exchange rate could still vary around the central rate, defined in basket terms, but the central rate itself changed by a pre-announced amount (the slope of the crawl) each day. The slope was the difference between the expected inflation rate in Israel and that of its partners; the crawl was one of the benefits of the new regime: The crawling band introduced de facto IT to Israel before it was officially introduced. The crawling band significantly reduced the frequency and magnitude of realignments, permitted smoother adjustment of the exchange rate, and lowered uncertainty regarding the real exchange rate.

From Crawling Band to Crawling Fan

Over time, pressures associated with increased capital mobility created a need for increased flexibility of the exchange rate. Although inflation was declining, this decline was a result of a disinflationary monetary policy requiring high nominal and real interest rates. Together with an improving geopolitical environment and strong economic growth, capital flows into Israel grew rapidly and exerted considerable upward pressure on the domestic currency. The level and width of the band (despite its widening in 1995) did not provide enough flexibility to avoid a clash between two conflicting goals: the rate of inflation and the exchange rate. The sheqel moved to the strong (lower) limit of the band, and the BoI was forced to defend the exchange rate band by buying foreign currency, in amounts and at a cost that threatened to become unsustainable. The ensuing costs of sterilization and desire to resolve conflicting goals led to the adoption of the crawling fan regime in June 1997.

The crawling fan was a response to the pressures generated by attempting to simultaneously target inflation and exchange rates by substantially increasing the actual and potential variability of the exchange rate. The slope of the lower (stronger domestic currency) limit of the band was reduced to 4 percent while the

to October 1991); a preannounced crawling peg (from October 1991 to May 1995); a crawling band that was widened in several steps (from May 1995 to July 1998); a de facto float with a formal wide crawling band (from August 1998 to April 2000); and a free float (since April 2000). The details of the evolution are presented in Table 8.

From Fixed Peg to the U.S. Dollar to a Basket Peg

The fixed peg to the dollar was adopted in January 1990 as part of the economic stabilization program of late 1989, but soon had to be adjusted. The single currency peg was aimed at reducing inflation quickly by delivering credibility to anti-inflationary policies. The inflation rate was indeed reduced rapidly from four-digit levels at the beginning of 1990 to 249.3 percent by end-1990 and 60.4 percent by end-1991. The significant progress in disinflation was irreversible, in part owing to the visibility of a fixed exchange rate and its impact on expectations, but was slower than targeted (the targets were 95 percent and 32 percent, respectively) because of the factors inherited from the centrally planned economy (for example, the indexation mechanisms and low confidence in the stability of the zloty). With inflation much higher in Poland than in its main trading partners, the zloty underwent a significant real appreciation, resulting in a rapid loss of price competitiveness; the initial current account surplus in 1990 was reversed and the deficit widened at a fast pace in 1991.

The move from the dollar peg to the basket peg was hence motivated mainly by concerns over loss of competitiveness. The widening of the current account deficit and the beginning of the decline in the level of official reserves were considered a significant risk factor to the stability of the exchange rate regime and the whole economy. Although the single currency peg provided transparency and helped anchor inflation expectations, it also led to exposure to changes in the value of the dollar, given the rapidly growing importance of trade with Western Europe. To reduce this exposure and address the loss of competitiveness, the zloty was pegged to a basket of five currencies in May 1991, with the basket reflecting the composition of Poland's international trade, and the central parity was devalued against the dollar. The basket peg introduced some flexibility by allowing variations in the zloty's value that reflected cross exchange rate movements vis-à-vis the dollar.

From Fixed Peg to Crawling Peg

The move from the fixed peg to a crawling peg was again motivated by competitiveness concerns. After the first two years of transition, the authorities recognized that relatively high inflation would persist for some

time and that inflation differentials combined with a fixed exchange rate would undermine external competitiveness. Maintaining competitiveness would call for further step devaluations that would result in uncertainty and distortion. The authorities also acknowledged, however, the need to maintain the peg to anchor inflation expectations. A preannounced crawling peg to a basket was introduced in October 1991, as a compromise between the goals of further disinflation and competitiveness. The basket was devalued according to a preannounced path at a constant pace on a daily basis. The rate of crawl was set at a level lower than the targeted inflation differential to support gradual disinflation and to smooth the path of real exchange rate appreciation; although the crawl rate was only gradually reduced from August 1993, two further step devaluations of the parity still proved necessary in 1992 and 1993 to address the loss of competitiveness.

From Preannounced Crawling Peg to Crawling Band

A large current account surplus and capital inflows with an increasingly open economy in the mid-1990s called for greater flexibility in the exchange rate. The zloty faced significant appreciation pressures from the current account surpluses in 1994–95, resulting mainly from a marked increase in net unclassified transactions associated with cross-border trade between Poland and its neighbors. At the same time, FDI inflows, persistently growing from the start of the transition, and nonresident portfolio investments from early 1995 added to the appreciation pressures. Portfolio inflows were attracted by the improving fundamentals of the Polish economy, as well as by a highly predictable exchange rate under the preannounced crawling peg that enabled foreign investors to easily estimate the forthcoming scale of zloty devaluation. The crawling peg therefore not only was unable to fully accommodate the appreciation pressure, but also added to it by attracting short-term inflows. The increased flexibility permitted in March 1995 by widening the NBP's bid-ask spread (from ±0.5 percent to ±2.0 percent) was not sufficient to address these pressures.

In mid-May 1995, the crawling band system was put in place, again as a compromise solution between keeping the exchange rate as an anchor and allowing some flexibility to respond to the persistent appreciation pressures from the FX inflows. The anchor role of the exchange rate under the crawling band mechanism was maintained by limiting the zloty's fluctuations within a band and letting the band crawl at a rate less than inflation differentials. The regime change was carried out without a major shift in the monetary policy framework, in which the NBP formally followed a monetary targeting strategy while de facto implementing an eclectic policy, focusing on both interest

Table 8. Evolution of Poland's Exchange Rate Regime since 1990

Date	Event
I. Administratively fixed exchange rate regime—hard peg (January 1990–October 1991)	
January 1, 1990	The zloty fixed to the U.S. dollar (PLN 0.95 = US$1)
May 17, 1991	The zloty fixed to a basket of five currencies (US$–45%, DEM–35%, GBP–10%, FRF and CHF–5%) and devalued against the U.S. dollar by 14.4%
II. Crawling peg regime (October 1991–May 1995)	
October 14, 1991	The crawling peg introduced (monthly rate of crawl: 1.8%) with a formal fluctuation band of ±2.0% and the National Bank of Poland (NBP)'s margin of ±0.5%
February 26, 1992	The zloty devalued against the basket by 12.0%
August 27, 1993	Monthly rate of crawl: 1.6%; the zloty devalued against the basket by 8.0%
September 13, 1994	Monthly rate of crawl: 1.5%
November 30, 1994	Monthly rate of crawl: 1.4%
February 16, 1995	Monthly rate of crawl: 1.2%
March 6, 1995	The NBP's margin increased to (2.0%
III. Crawling band regime (May 1995–July 1998)	
May 16, 1995	Fluctuation band increased to ±7.0%; NBP intervenes in the foreign exchange (FX) market both directly[1] and indirectly[2]
December 22, 1995	Revaluation of the central parity rate by 6.0%
January 8, 1996	Monthly rate of crawl: 1.0%
February 26, 1998	Monthly rate of crawl: 0.8%; fluctuation band increased to ±10.0% and reduction in the scale of direct FX interventions
July 17, 1998	Monthly rate of crawl: 0.65%
July 31, 1998	Final abolition of direct interventions on the FX market
IV. De facto floating (August 1998–April 2000)	
September 10, 1998	Monthly rate of crawl: 0.5%
October 13, 1998	Public commitment by the MPC to float the zloty at a future date (press conference at which the *Medium-Term Strategy of Monetary Policy (1999-2003)* was presented)
October 29, 1998	Fluctuation band increased to −12.5%
January 1, 1999	New currency basket (EUR–55%, US$–45%)
March 25, 1999	Monthly rate of crawl: 0.3%; fluctuation band increased to ±15.0%
June 7, 1999	Abolition of fixing transactions (indirect interventions)
V. Floating exchange rate regime (since April 2000)	
April 12, 2000	Formal introduction of the floating exchange rate regime

Source: Polański (2004, p. 14).
Note: DEM refers to the deutsche mark, GBP refers to the pound sterling, FRF refers to the French franc, and CHF refers to the Swiss franc.
[1]Direct interventions were typical, market-based central bank interventions.
[2]Indirect interventions were FX transactions with commercial banks during fixing sessions.

rates and exchange rate control aimed at achieving a continued gradual disinflation.

Effectively, however, the crawling band system provided less flexibility than envisaged initially. Under this system, the central rate of the zloty continued to be devalued every business day by a certain amount. While the market rate was officially allowed to fluctuate within a band of ±7.0 percent, the NBP used a one-sided inner intervention band on the appreciation side. The NBP purchases of foreign exchange (both through market interventions and by fixing transactions) resulted in a massive increase in official reserves during 1995. In addition, in light of the high interest rate differential, intervention purchases led to high sterilization costs. The sustained appreciation pressure on the zloty induced the central bank to further revise its regime; in September 1995, the NBP moved its unofficial intervention level from about 5 percent to about 6 percent (on the strong side of the band) from the central rate, and in December 1995, it revalued the zloty against the basket by 6 percent.

Persistent appreciation pressure on the zloty and the widening current account deficit during 1996 led to a further increase in the flexibility of the exchange rate. Also mindful of the potential consequences for financial stability of growing capital mobility, the NBP abandoned its unofficial intervention level in May 1997 and allowed the volatility of the zloty to increase within the formal ±7.0 percent fluctuation band. As under the crawling peg system, the disinflation policy was intended to be supported by a reduction in the rate of crawl of the central parity.

From Crawling Band to De Facto and De Jure Free Float

The transition to greater exchange flexibility accelerated considerably from February 1998 as a consequence of a monetary policy regime change and the need for faster disinflation. As the new 1997 Polish constitution and the NBP Act gave the sole responsibility for the conduct of monetary policy to the central bank (goal independence included), the newly created Monetary Policy Council (MPC) decided to adopt the IT framework and committed itself to gradually float the zloty. IT combined with a floating exchange rate was considered to be the best framework to address the challenges facing Poland, that is, completing disinflation at the time of a growing current account deficit and increasing capital mobility.

In particular, with increasing capital mobility, competitiveness and disinflation objectives became increasingly incompatible under the eclectic monetary policy strategy, inducing the NBP to introduce further steps toward a floating exchange rate. By maintaining the exchange rate within preannounced limits and reducing exchange rate risk for financial investors, the crawling band system continued to attract large capital inflows. The inflows required interventions and a greater need for sterilization to neutralize their monetary impact. The interest rate policy aimed at restraining inflation resulted in significant sterilization costs, while attracting additional capital inflows and slowing down the disinflation process.

Given the unstable international environment and Poland's growing current account deficit, the NBP moved to a de facto floating regime during 1998–99. The fluctuation band was widened in several steps to ±15 percent in March 1999 and its crawl rate was reduced in several steps. The volume of FX interventions was also reduced (just before the Russian crisis, the NBP withdrew from direct FX interventions, letting the zloty absorb the contagion effects), and fixing transactions were eliminated in June 1999. The NBP has not intervened in the FX market since, although it continued to announce the central parity and the fluctuation band. In the final phase of the crawling band system, the zloty was hence fluctuating freely within a band of 30 percent, with no NBP intervention.

The considerable widening of the band width and further reductions in the pace of the central parity devaluation reduced the significance of the band. However, the existing band could still be considered as a potential commitment of the NBP to influence the FX market. After the required consultations with the government,[13] the free float regime was adopted officially on April 12, 2000—a step considered as the formal confirmation of a de facto switch to the floating system. Following this decision, the NBP ceased to announce the central parity and the fluctuation band, because the latter could constitute a target for speculation in an environment of large capital flows and a very high current account deficit. This action constituted the key step in the process of introducing a full-fledged IT regime, and there has been no NBP intervention in the FX market since then.

Coordination of the Regime Transition with Supporting Elements

The gradual move to flexibility was supported by structural reforms that strengthened sustainability and credibility of the transition. Integration with supporting steps was vital for a coherent transition process to a free float while avoiding policy reversals.

Monetary Operations and Development of Financial Markets

Financial markets have been developing since the beginning of the economic transition, particularly from the second half of the 1990s, helping to increase the efficiency of monetary operations and reducing the role of exchange rate policy in the disinflation process. The first market to develop was the interbank deposit market, which facilitated banks' management of their liquidity. The existence of a well-functioning deposit market was a precondition for the introduction of mod-

---

[13]According to the 1997 NBP Act, the change in the foreign exchange system (unlike its parameters, such as the rate of crawl and the width of the band) had to be agreed on by the government.

ern market operations to implement monetary policy. The subsequent development of the treasury bill market enabled the government to fund budget deficits and provided securities that could be used for interbank and monetary operations. Effective monetary operations facilitated transmission of monetary policy to inflation through market interest rates. The introduction of partial convertibility of the zloty resulted in the emergence of the interbank FX market in the early 1990s. The Warsaw Stock Exchange, established in April 1991, developed simultaneously with the interbank markets.

The central bank contributed to the development of the financial markets mainly by creating infrastructure and institutions, setting standards, and creating incentives for market participants. The system of unified bank accounts in the NBP, which was crucial for the money market, was established in 1993–94, facilitating the introduction of averaging in the required reserve system at end-1994. The payment system was developed simultaneously. The NBP supported market development with the early introduction of repurchase operations in 1993. A book-entry system for treasury bills and NBP bills was introduced in 1995. The NBP (in cooperation with commercial banks) promoted the setting of market standards and encouraged banks to engage in market operations. In 1993, the money market dealers system was introduced. In 1994, the NBP started to reissue NBP money bills, which became the main tool for open market operations.[14] A deep and liquid interbank deposit market developed following these measures. The reference WIBOR-WIBID rates became reliable market indicators, providing reference prices for settlement in derivative instruments.

The development of the domestic financial markets accelerated in the mid-1990s, with the rapid growth in the scale of transactions and turnover. The latter was stimulated by the presence of foreign investors attracted by improving economic fundamentals and a successful accord with the London Club. The domestic financial markets became increasingly liquid and offered a wide spectrum of instruments for financial management. The stimulus to the development of the bond market was also supported by declining inflation, which allowed the government to limit the issues of short-term bills and floaters and to increase the issues of fixed rate bonds; the maturity of the public debt was extended; and the first international placement was conducted in 1995. The development of the spot FX market accelerated with the crawling band from 1995. Since 1998, a vibrant market for FX swaps became the most liquid component of the domestic money market. The growing international integration of the domestic financial markets gave domestic entities access to derivative markets abroad, which offered hedging against price risk in the bond market.

Foreign Exchange and Derivatives Markets

In Poland, the FX market was developed in conjunction with the other financial markets and was supported by the scope for exchange rate volatility provided by greater exchange rate flexibility. The crawling peg system adopted at the end of 1991 permitted very limited exchange rate flexibility. Until 1995, the NBP acted as the sole market maker in the interbank FX market. The introduction of the crawling band in 1995 was a stimulus for development of the spot market, as well as for the rise of the forward FX market that in turn has facilitated hedging against FX risks. Whereas the spot FX market had already been well developed by 1998, when the NBP ceased its interventions, derivatives markets developed more gradually, with a significant pickup in the year before the float.

In developing hedging markets for foreign exchange, the authorities have faced the typical trade-off between the benefits and risks associated with the use of derivative instruments. Although acknowledging that increased availability of hedging instruments would help economic agents cope with increasing exchange rate risks, they also recognized the risk that derivative transactions could facilitate speculation. In fact, there were fears that forward transactions could allow speculative attacks and would be harder to control (use of derivatives indeed augmented the appreciation pressure on the zloty in 1998). The authorities hence considered it important to develop derivatives markets cautiously, with liberalization taking place only at later stages of the move to flexibility.

The authorities also recognized, however, that it would be difficult to stop the development of such markets as long as there were incentives and needs for such transactions. As in Israel, in most cases the pressures were created when discrepancies existed between economic fundamentals and the policy regime, and the latter was adjusted to reduce these discrepancies. It was recognized that it would be hard to stop the development of derivatives once the markets for underlying instruments (for example, treasury bills and treasury bonds) were liberalized. In fact, maintaining restrictions on derivative transactions was considered to be potentially counterproductive, leading to an even faster development of derivatives offshore in an attempt to circumvent onshore restrictions. A vibrant zloty NDF market indeed emerged in London, in part reflecting the restrictions on derivative transactions in the domestic market.

The authorities hence moved to liberalize FX swap markets, while also having some safeguards in place. In 1998, the Ministry of Finance issued a favorable

---

[14]Issuing money bills was considered to be a more effective way to absorb excess liquidity than, for example, deposit auctions, because a secondary market for these bills emerged, facilitating liquidity redistribution within the banking sector.

Nature and Pace of the Exit

Although the macroeconomic imbalances had been building gradually, the transition to the float took place very quickly, with the collapse of the peg and the outbreak of economic turmoil. After having reached a historical maximum in April 1998, international reserves were almost halved by the speculative attacks, with the loss of confidence compounded by the default of a state government on its foreign agreements. The significant loss of reserves led to an attempt to adjust the exchange rate bands and introduce the so-called endogenous diagonal band. Under the new system, the inner exchange rate bands were abandoned, and the new bands were adjusted every three working days according to the behavior of the exchange rate over the previous three days. With the exchange rate rapidly moving to the upper limit of the new band and a continued loss of reserves, the new system was abandoned in two days: on January 15, 1999, the CBB announced that it would not intervene in the market, and on the subsequent working day it introduced the floating exchange rate system.

The switch to a float was accompanied by a short period of sharp depreciation of the currency and great macroeconomic uncertainty. The sharp depreciation of the currency in less than three weeks caused significant market panic, given the relatively recent history of high inflation in Brazil. The crisis, however, was not accompanied by generalized and severe financial distress in the private sector. In contrast to similar crises in other countries in the period, the turmoil did not result in a banking crisis or widespread bankruptcy in the nonfinancial sector, owing to the limited exposure of the private sector to exchange rate depreciation. Putting together an alternative monetary policy framework relatively quickly helped limit market and monetary instability.

Coordinating the Transition with Supporting Elements of Flexibility

There was no advance coordination with other elements to support the transition to a floating system, but the switch took place rapidly and with a relatively short period of instability. Although many observers characterized Brazil's exit as a "preannounced crisis," no exit strategy had been developed in advance with deliberate attempts to put in place the elements to facilitate the transition. Nevertheless, some advances made in the preceding years—although not meant to prepare for a transition to a floating exchange rate—were important for a softer landing. In particular, improvements in monetary, financial, and fiscal sectors prevented a deeper crisis and eased the transition to the new regime.

The Real Plan had generated, for the first time in decades, a low-inflation environment. Considering its historical pattern, the Brazilian economy had enjoyed a relatively long period of stabilization (four years), which had somehow changed agents' behavior. For instance, the pervasive indexation system had been undermined. Had the depreciation occurred closer to the start of the stabilization, the fears of the return of high inflation would perhaps have been more well founded.

The FX market was relatively well developed, though with a dual market structure until recently. The spot FX market traded substantial volumes with high liquidity. The futures market was developed as well, but other derivatives contracts (options, swaps, and forwards) were traded at low volumes. Higher exchange rate uncertainty resulting from the float helped stimulate the derivatives markets. In the context of the first steps toward capital account liberalization, the authorities introduced at end-1988 a floating exchange rate market, alongside the commercial or free exchange rate market. Although most transactions were carried out in the other official market when the real was floated, the new market acted as an important reference point in the process of capital account liberalization, with the goal of bringing FX operations in the parallel market into a regulated market. In fact, the regulation increasingly broadened the operations that could go through the new market. As a result, the parallel market lost its economic significance, with a significant fall in the exchange rate spread over the official market. The two official markets were unified shortly after the float (formally unified only in 2005).

The pattern of direct intervention in the FX market has changed with the new exchange rate regime. During the crawling peg, the CBB intervened within inner bands through spread auctions, alongside the usual sale and purchase auctions. The spread auctions were the main instrument used to set the pace of devaluations and were usually held at regular intervals. The magnitude of balance of payments net flows led the CBB to intervene in the market quite frequently and on both sides. The size of the inner bands was marginally increased during 1998, and the adjustment pace of the bands also rose slightly. When the real was floated, the CBB announced that interventions would be occasional and limited, aiming to curb disorderly exchange rate movements. In fact, the interventions became less frequent and were not meant to achieve any specific target. However, during the second semesters of 2001 and 2002 (periods of pronounced market pressures), the interventions were more frequent and systematic.[2] In 2004, the CBB announced a policy of replenishing international reserves, taking advantage of favorable market conditions and attempting neither to add undue

---

[2]In mid-2001, the CBB announced a daily sale of US$50 million in the foreign exchange market that lasted until December. In March 2002, the CBB began to conduct exchange swap operations.

volatility to the market nor to impede the fluctuation of the real. No commitment was made to a precise rule as to amounts and timing of intervention, or to a predefined reserve target.

Nevertheless, indirect mechanisms of FX market intervention played a key role in both regimes. The government issued U.S.-dollar-linked debt to ease demand pressures on the exchange rate market, providing also a hedge to the private sector. The share of dollar-linked debt in the federal domestic debt rose significantly, from 5.3 percent in 1995 to 20.9 percent in 1998, causing the government to incur a predominant part of the financial cost of the depreciation. The CBB also engaged in transactions in the futures market during the peg system. In the 1999 agreement with the IMF, however, the government committed to refrain from using futures market operations. Under the new regime, it issued securities with an exchange swap transaction during the period of market pressures in 2002. Coupled with the exchange rate depreciation of the period, these operations led the dollar-linked debt to reach a maximum share of 41 percent of federal domestic debt that year. With the recovery of confidence and the policy to reduce such debt—including the conduct of reverse exchange swap operations—its share fell to 1.2 percent at end-2005.

The financial system was in reasonably good condition at the time of the float, after having undergone a large adjustment in previous years to adapt to the low-inflation environment. As a consequence of the stabilization, financial institutions had to adjust considerably, with some of the financial institutions, including large banks, facing significant difficulties. However, under the Program of Incentives to the Restructuring and Strengthening of the National Financial System launched in 1995, the private financial system was restructured through mergers and acquisitions by foreign banks and some liquidations. By the time the peg system collapsed, private financial institutions had already completed the adjustment. At that time, the state-owned bank segment was also undergoing a process of restructuring through the Program for Reducing the Presence of the State Public Sector in Banking Activity.

Moreover, the financial system was not dollarized, reflecting mainly a number of FX regulations that limited a pronounced exposure to FX risks.[3] Banking deposits or payments in foreign currency were not permitted. External loans, in turn, were on-lent with obligatory dollar-indexed clauses, avoiding problems of mismatching between assets and liabilities. Hence, the depreciation of the domestic currency during the crisis exit did not produce significant losses. In fact, the financial system was not exposed to risks associated with an exchange rate depreciation; many financial institutions were trading against the sustainability of the bands through derivatives contracts so that they were exposed to risks associated with an appreciation of the domestic currency.

Prudential regulations against FX risks that require financial institutions to hold capital against that risk were not in place at the time of the float. There were limits on the amounts of foreign currency purchased and sold in the spot market, but no limit on the global exchange rate risk exposure of financial institutions.[4] Positions in the derivatives market were not considered. Given a long history with pegged exchange rates and the steady adjustment of the exchange rate in previous years, market participants were not accustomed to assessing, as a matter of routine, the exchange rate risks posed by regular market volatility. A few months after the crisis, the monetary authorities set forth specific regulations limiting the exposure of financial institutions to exchange rate risks.

The nonfinancial private sector was, nevertheless, not exposed to unhedged exchange rate risks, whereas the public sector was vulnerable to depreciation of the real. Although the nonfinancial private sector had increased its external debt, it benefited from hedging mechanisms, such as foreign currency proceeds in the case of exporters, large remittance of flows abroad prior to the collapse of the peg system, the issuance of domestic dollar-linked public debt, and the derivative transactions. In fact, private agents benefited from those hedging mechanisms with the depreciation. Some private agents were exposed to exchange risks through dollar-linked leasing contracts, but those operations were not significant in the system. In contrast, the public sector was financially vulnerable to a depreciation because of the issuance of external debt, domestic dollar-indexed securities, and derivative transactions. As a result, the government incurred most of the financial distress.

The monetary policy institutional framework had advanced in the period before the float, and additional improvements were made following the adoption of IT as the alternative monetary policy framework. The CBB had created the Monetary Policy Committee (Copom) in June 1996, and the minutes of its meetings began being published in March 1998. However, there was a need for greater transparency and further progress in ensuring the CBB's operational independence. Significant progress was achieved with the adoption of IT. In particular, the level of transparency has increased, and the CBB has gained greater credibility. Although price

---

[3]During the high-inflation period, a widespread and sophisticated indexation system avoided financial disintermediation and the dollarization of the economy.

[4]There was a specific limit on long positions (amounts exceeding those limits should be deposited in the CBB) and a limit contingent on banks' adjusted net worth for short positions, both in the spot market. The limits on the short position in the spot market were abolished in October 1999 and on the long position at the end of 2005. For the prudential regulation on the foreign exchange market in Brazil, see Loyola (2005).

stability appears among other central bank objectives in the legislation enacted in 1965, in practice it became its primary commitment over time. De jure central bank independence has not been adopted, although the CBB has been de facto independent in conducting monetary policy.

Monetary policy instruments and the capacity to affect interest rates were well developed before the float and were further improved in the transition. The government securities market was already well developed at the time, with substantial trading volumes and high liquidity supporting monetary operations. During the peg system, Copom set targets for two interest rates on discount loans, which, by arbitrage, led to the formation of the Selic overnight interest rate—the benchmark rate (the rate on overnight repurchase (repo) operations between banks, with government securities as collateral). Greater use was made of open market operations in conducting monetary policy during 1998. The CBB suspended both rates following the float. In March 1999, it began setting targets for the Selic rate, determined by its interventions instead of banks' arbitrage operations. The Selic rate has worked as the main reference for the other interest rates in the economy.

The transition to the floating exchange rate system took place in the context of a fairly open capital account. Brazil had gradually liberalized its capital account during the 1990s. The abundance of capital inflows led to the adoption of some restrictive measures on inflows from 1993 through 1996, but the authorities started relaxing these measures in 1997. In addition, further measures were adopted in those years to liberalize outflows, with a view to reducing net inflows without affecting the trend toward greater integration with financial markets. After the float, further liberalizing measures were introduced.[5] Brazil accepted the obligations of IMF Article of Agreement VIII in November 1999.

Challenges during the Transition

The main challenges the monetary authorities faced during the transition were to curb market panic, restore foreign investors' confidence, and prevent the return of high inflation. The authorities considered it important

[5]These measures included, for instance, reduction and subsequent elimination of the minimum maturity requirements for external loans and reduction to zero percent of the financial transaction tax on foreign investment in fixed-income funds and on external loans with an average maturity above 90 days in 1999; regulation of investment in the financial and capital markets (nonresidents were allowed to invest in the same instruments as were residents); consolidation of the regulation on external loans and debt securities in 2000 (ending the CBB prior approval requirement); permission for prepayment of external debt and regulation of the issuance of real-denominated external debt in 2004; and more direct procedures and clearer rules for the conversion of domestic currency into foreign currency in 2005 (for more details, see Goldfajn and Minella, 2005).

to limit the period of high uncertainty and attain a return of capital inflows to reverse the overshooting of the exchange rate and resume external financing and foreign investment in the economy. The exchange rate depreciation, the absence of an anchor for inflation expectations, and memories of the high-inflation period fueled fears of a return to high inflation. Analysts predicted a double-digit inflation rate for that year, with some forecasts reaching as high as 80 percent, with considerable uncertainty about the pass-through of the exchange rate to prices.

The adoption of IT that shortly followed the float contributed significantly to limiting the period of uncertainty and to preventing the return of high inflation following the depreciation. In a joint statement with the IMF in February 1999, the authorities declared that they intended to put in place an IT system. In March, the government announced that the goal would be to bring inflation down to a single-digit annualized rate by the last quarter of 1999, and that the IT regime would be adopted by the end of June. In fact, IT was implemented as scheduled within a period of six months. The targets were set for 1999, 2000, and 2001.

At the time of the float, IT was considered to be the best alternative to play a key role in anchoring inflation expectations and reducing uncertainties in the economy. Keeping the peg system with a simple change in the exchange rate value would not be appropriate, because the peg system had lost market trust. It would also be hard to gauge the appropriate level for the exchange rate peg because of the imbalances and uncertainties surrounding the economy. On the other hand, excessive devaluation would have brought about unnecessary inflationary pressures. A fully discretionary policy without an explicit anchor would not be suitable in the context of high uncertainties, a history of high inflation, and weaknesses in monetary institutions.

The government also had to put in place a new fiscal policy regime aimed at stabilizing the economy and preventing a return to high inflation. The economic slowdown and some fiscal tightening that had started in 1998 had already contributed to restraining the magnitude of the exchange rate pass-through to inflation. In addition to the end-1998 measures, new restrictive fiscal measures were introduced in 1999 as part of a new policy mix with three pillars (IT, a floating exchange rate, and a sound fiscal policy), signaling a major shift in the fiscal regime. The fiscal adjustment also had to cope with the fiscal effects of the currency depreciation. In fact, the economic turmoil, which exposed the fiscal fragility of the economy, created better political conditions for a turnaround in fiscal policy. As a result, the primary surplus rose by 3.3 percentage points of GDP during 1999. The primary fiscal surplus has reached record highs recently—a continuation of the policy initiated during the transition period.

These efforts were also supported by a tightening of monetary policy, external financial support, and government efforts to normalize relations with investors. The CBB raised the base interest rate substantially after the depreciation. As the macroeconomic situation improved, the interest rate hikes were reversed and monetary policy gradually became less restrictive. The revised IMF-supported program in November 1999 pioneered the use of inflation targets as part of the program conditionalities. On the external side, the financial package from the IMF played a key role, also by helping to restore capital flows. The government's active relations with international banks and investors also helped in major international banks' maintaining trade and interbank lines in the country. The government also gave the reassurance that the capital account liberalization trend would not be reversed. Capital flows resumed as the panic was reversed and macro conditions improved.[6]

The implementation of IT nevertheless encountered several challenges. First, the system was adopted in a period of great uncertainty and sharp exchange rate depreciation. Second, its goal was not simply to maintain the inflation rate at low levels, but to bring it down. Third, the new framework was part of a process of building the credibility of the monetary authority and developing monetary institutions. Fourth, it was necessary, in a short period, to build a technical capacity, including forecasting models. The monetary transmission mechanisms were not well understood and estimated. Brazil had enjoyed less than five years of stabilization, so only a short sample size was available to accurately estimate inflation dynamics, particularly given the structural shifts in the macroeconomic policy regime. Coherent conduct of monetary policy under the IT regime, intensive communication efforts (publication of a quarterly Inflation Report and timely release of Copom minutes), and investing in research and modeling at the CBB helped in addressing the challenges.

Lessons from the Brazilian Experience

Although Brazil's transition to a floating regime took place in the context of an economic crisis, as a whole, the policy response to the crisis was successful. The following lessons can be drawn from the Brazilian experience:

• A pegged exchange rate system that generates increasing external imbalances and is coupled with an unsound fiscal policy would not be sustainable.

• A transition to a floating exchange rate system should be planned to avoid the risk of being caught unprepared, and should be accompanied by the announcement and possibly implementation of the new regime to replace the exchange rate anchor.

• A transition to a floating system in a situation of fiscal and external imbalances leads to a high degree of uncertainty, calling for tight fiscal and monetary policy.

• A financial system with low exposure to exchange rate risks, coupled with prudential regulation that deals with such risk, contributes to a softer landing after a crisis exit.

• The adoption of IT could be essential to establishing a new credible monetary regime that preserves stabilization gains previously achieved, in particular in the context of uncertainty and developing monetary institutions.

• Although more advanced planning for the implementation of IT could have resulted in a smoother transition, it was possible to implement the new framework rapidly and successfully, owing to both the determination of the CBB to put in place the essential elements that comprise a full-fledged IT regime and the supportive fiscal policy.

Czech Republic (1996–97)[7]

The Czech Republic abandoned its horizontal band regime in June 1997 without an exit strategy and after a mini currency crisis that came as a reaction to a number of macroeconomic and structural policy-related factors. The mix of an expansionary fiscal and contractionary monetary policy, along with the slow progress in structural reforms, became inconsistent with the pegged regime in an open economy with a largely liberalized capital account. The authorities managed a soft landing after the crisis, which provided an opportunity to change the overall macroeconomic management. In the short period that followed the exit, IT was chosen as the only available option for the new nominal anchor. Although incomplete preparedness for IT contributed to the challenges faced in the early stages, its introduction in a reasonably short period helped limit prolonged market instability and lessened the severity of the disorderly exit. IT has also proved successful in achieving price stability and anchoring inflation under a floating regime.

---

[6]The combination of tighter fiscal and monetary policies, adoption of IT, and external financial support was crucial to reverse inflation expectations and bring inflation down (in early 2000, inflation expectations fell below 7 percent). After peaking in early 1999, the inflation rate fell and the real was stabilized. In mid-1999, the panic was reversed (Fraga, 2000). These improvements allowed interest rate cuts from April 1999.

[7]Prepared by David Vávra (Czech National Bank). The author thanks Miroslav Hrncir, Tomas Kvapil, Vera Masindova, Ivana Matalikova, and Rudolf Olsovsky for insightful comments and discussions.

Factors Triggering the Exit

The exchange rate peg, in effect from the beginning of the transition process, provided a useful nominal anchor in the early periods of transition, but became increasingly difficult to sustain as integration with international markets continued. The basket peg within a ±0.5 percent band helped stabilize inflation after price liberalization while providing for a competitiveness cushion through an initially depreciated parity. Inflation quickly fell and the economy soon began recovering from a slowdown associated with the transition process. Monetary policy was able to retain independence under monetary targeting (M2). As the transition progressed, however, the exchange system was liberalized at a fast pace, with gradual relaxation of surrender requirements, easing of administrative procedures for capital account transactions, and full current account convertibility in 1995. With the Czech Republic becoming the first former socialist OECD member in 1996, deadlines were established for phasing out the remaining capital controls.

The opening of the economy brought large capital inflows, with a significant volatile short-term component, exposing monetary policy to the "impossible trinity" dilemma. These flows began putting appreciation pressure on the exchange rate in the 1993–95 period, prompting the monetary authorities to resort to large-scale sterilization policies, in an attempt to maintain simultaneously the exchange rate and monetary targets. Yet, money targets were repeatedly missed and progress in disinflation slowed.

As a partial response to these developments, the exchange rate band was widened (to ±7.5 percent) in February 1996, but this provided only a temporary relief in the absence of a needed change in the policy mix. Greater exchange rate flexibility helped in reversing short-term flows in 1996, by introducing more uncertainty into short-term speculative investments, and provided monetary policy with more room for maneuvering. In the absence of a countercyclical policy reaction, however, the macroeconomic situation became unsustainable: With the slow progress in economic restructuring and corporate governance, the economy started overheating, disinflation slowed down, and the external balance deteriorated.[8] In the absence of a sufficiently tight fiscal policy to contain domestic and external imbalances, monetary policy was tightened

from 1996, attracting additional short-term inflows that put further pressure on the exchange rate. With deteriorating economic fundamentals and the lack of steady long-term capital inflows, the sustainability of the peg became hostage to a potential reversal of short-term capital inflows.

The Nature of the Exit

The Czech Republic's switch from the exchange rate band could be characterized as a mini-crisis exit following a temporary capital flight. With the exchange rate being at the appreciating limit of the band, that the koruna would depreciate effectively became a one-way bet, because it was considered unlikely that the strong edge of the band would be relaxed, given the large current account deficits (Begg, 1998). Rising political instability, combined with contagion from the Asian crisis, induced investors to abandon the region, including the Czech Republic, which had been receiving significant amounts of short-term capital inflows.

Despite the circumstances, the crisis was not severe and was well managed. Exchange rate overshooting was avoided (the koruna depreciated by a mere 13 percent), reserves loss was minimal (only about 20 percent of reserves was used to defend the peg and was soon replenished), and interest rates started to ease shortly (having more than doubled previously). Crucially, there was no spillover to the banking and financial sector. Moreover, the peg regime was not defended at all costs. The decision to float was announced rather quickly at a relatively calm moment during the crisis and was followed by an announcement of the intention to focus on long-term price stability. The authorities also announced temporary indicative bands for the exchange rate under an officially declared managed float. The market calmed down after these announcements.

Although not planned in advance, the exit was reasonably smooth. The authorities subsequently took important measures to improve the macroeconomic management, including by reducing fiscal imbalances, addressing labor market imbalances, launching a program for attracting FDI, and speeding up structural reforms, including privatization of the banking sector (Hrncir, 1998). Adoption of the inflation target as the new nominal anchor and implementation of IT as the new monetary policy framework played an important role in limiting the severity of the crisis following the exit.

Coordination with Supporting Elements of a Flexible Exchange Rate Regime

Being an abrupt exit in the context of a currency crisis, the switch out of the peg was not associated with any particular strategy to prepare the economy

---

[8]See, for example, Begg (1998) and Christensen (2004). Although domestic demand expansion, not the low level of competitiveness (exports continued to grow at high rates in that period), was the primary contributor to the worsening of the current account, the rapid deterioration of the various competitiveness indicators undermined the sustainability of the economic fundamentals. Falling corporate profitability also put in doubt the stability of the largely state-controlled banking system, which tended to support specific industries.

for flexible exchange rates. Although the sustainability of the peg had been in doubt for some time (at least since the monetary tightening in late 1996), no specific exit plan, in particular an alternative monetary policy framework to replace the peg, had been put in place. Some exchange rate flexibility had been introduced through a widening of the horizontal band before the crisis, but the move was under market pressure and not part of a deliberate process of establishing the supporting elements of a new monetary policy regime.

After a short period of heavily managed floating with Czech National Bank interventions on both sides of the indicative band, and rising inflation, IT was adopted as the new monetary policy regime. With various forms of pegged exchange rate regimes largely discredited and monetary targeting operationally difficult with a poor track record, IT was viewed to be the only feasible option. Because there were no deliberate plans to move to targeting inflation, only some, though key, conditions for successful IT implementation were in place at the time of its adoption (central bank operational independence, effective implementation of monetary policy, availability of a key policy rate, reasonably developed financial markets, and no fiscal dominance). Some of the other important conditions were absent (for example, price stability mandate, political and/or public support, a strong state-owned banking system, adequate capacity for forecasting inflation, accountability, and transparency), which in turn contributed to the challenges in regaining credibility in the early stages of the new regime.

One of the key elements in place to support the implementation of both IT and a floating exchange rate regime was reasonably well developed financial markets. At the time of the float, there were active spot and derivatives markets in foreign exchange. Interbank money markets and secondary markets for securities were sufficiently developed by mid-1994, so that the CNB could abandon its market-maker role, conduct repo operations through the open market, and modify its operative target from monetary base to banking reserves. By late 1995, the markets (though somewhat undermined by banking sector segmentation and other problems) were functioning sufficiently well to permit monetary transmission by targeting money market interest rates.

The CNB contributed significantly to the development of the financial markets. A major boom in FX market development took place in 1996, supported in part by the widening of the horizontal band and relaxation of impediments on bank-client and forward transactions. Market participants learned to work with FX risks, because small exchange rate fluctuations had been allowed early on, and especially following the significant widening of the band in 1996. The CNB actively promoted money market liquidity in the early 1990s by issuing its own bills, with the liquidity of the treasury-bill market largely constrained by near-balanced budgets during this period. It also coordinated issues of the bills of other government agencies, as well as encouraged market development by initially playing a market-maker role. A number of technical measures were taken to improve the market infrastructure, such as setting up a system of quoting interbank offered rates, establishing an online clearing center, and defining the legal basis for repo contracts.

The capacity to implement monetary policy was relatively advanced at the time of the exit, facilitating the operation of the new monetary framework with a floating exchange rate. The central bank had established reasonable capacity to affect short-term interest rates, one of the key supporting conditions for IT. The CNB adopted a gradual approach to changing its operational target from the monetary base to banking reserves, and subsequently to money market rates, following closely the development of the markets and instruments. With relatively well developed money and financial markets, the CNB began using short-term market interest rates as the operational variable in early 1996.[9] The CNB had a large variety of instruments for both active and passive operations.[10] The elements of an interest rate corridor emerged in 1997, but it was finalized only in 2001 (with a two-week repo rate supported by a stand-by deposit and lending facility). The importance of the role of required reserves fell rapidly given the reduced need for sterilization under the float. Many of the other existing instruments were abolished or consolidated to ensure compatibility with the new system.[11]

The financial system was also reasonably stable, with adequate capacity to manage FX risks. This stability likely helped avoid a spillover of the currency market pressures into the banking system, notwithstanding the presence of some vulnerabilities in the banking sector (Box 2). The agents had capacity and tools to manage FX risks, because the authorities had actively promoted market development for some time, including during the

---

[9]Banking reserves replaced the monetary base as the operational target in the second half of 1994, when the CNB stopped playing the role of market maker. This was designed as an intermediate stage before interest rate targeting could be implemented, in particular to facilitate daily liquidity management without jeopardizing the stability of the underdeveloped money market. During 1995, the reserve-based system was complemented with conditions on the limits of market interest rate increases, and from late 1995 with an indicative corridor.

[10]Market-based instruments played a dominant role from early 1993, but repo operations fully replaced refinancing credit auctions only after the secondary short-term bill market was reasonably developed in mid-1994.

[11]Operations at the three-month maturity were abandoned in 2001, because the demand was small and markets were unclear about the CNB's price-taking behavior at this longer maturity. Refinancing operations at the discount rate were also abolished in 1996, with the CNB considering such operations as nonsystematic, supporting liquidity of problematic banks at below-market rates, or supporting certain (export) industries.

Box 2. Czech Republic: The Condition of the Financial System

The Czech financial system came through the foreign exchange (FX) crisis largely unscathed, notwithstanding some ongoing vulnerabilities in the banking sector. The main reason for the good performance of the banking system during the crisis was its good capacity to manage FX risks, acquired in the preceding period. The banks reacted promptly to the changing situation using their standard information and decision-making systems to limit losses by engaging in more active liquidity management, closing FX positions daily, imposing credit restrictions, and more frequently changing deposit and FX conversion rates for their clients; in fact, FX transactions during the crisis had a positive impact on profits in a vast majority of banks, and the sector had been very profitable in 1997 overall, also thanks to the performance during the crisis period. There was no worsening of the loan quality associated with the crisis, because the exposure through FX-denominated loans was either covered by foreign currency proceeds (that is, with positions naturally hedged) or through hedging instruments, or such loans were provided only to first-rate clients (usually of foreign banking institutions). The situation was also helped by a relatively smooth management of the crisis and the limited depreciation of the exchange rate.

Although insulated from the FX crisis contagion, the banking system was in a state of flux in the mid-1990s, mostly owing to solvency problems in the small banks segment and to slow progress in major bank privatizations. As a whole, the banking system was inefficient and noncompetitive; the levels of intermediation and maturity transformation were very low, with large spreads. Credit markets were highly segmented and uncompetitive at the time of the exit; as late as in 2000, private sector credit to GDP was well below the relevant market economy benchmark and the quality of the legal environment lagged significantly behind that of neighboring countries (OECD, 1996; Buiter and Taci, 2003; Christensen, 2004; and Arvai, 2005). As in other transition countries, the absence of long-term instruments contributed much to the large volumes of direct foreign borrowing and other capital inflows. Because the banking system development was relationship-based, with banks as the main financiers of the economic recovery, the slow privatization progress of banks also contributed to inefficient corporate control in the economy as a whole. The stagnation of structural reforms impacted the quality of the bank's loan portfolio.

The strengthening of the prudential and regulatory framework was gradual throughout the 1990s, and in general not directly associated with greater flexibility of the exchange rate. Although the FX risk exposure was regulated by the limits established on banks' open positions from the early 1990s and later was complemented by limits on short positions (to limit inflows of speculative capital),

both measures were considered as monetary rather than prudential. The strengthening of the framework began in late 1993, involving tougher licensing and asset classification conditions, adaptation of international and European Union (EU)–compatible accounting standards, restrictions on investment in certain sectors, and the requirement to make capital provisions on anticipated portfolio losses. Although the Czech National Bank had kept limits on banks' open FX positions from the early 1990s, other FX-risk-related prudential regulations, including a regulation that established capital adequacy rules for foreign exchange risks, came into effect only in 2000.

In addition to exogenous factors, such as the Basel Accords and EU harmonization requirements, the prudential and supervisory measures evolved according to the situation in the banking system. The stability of the banking system suffered from relatively loose and liberal conditions in the early 1990s. Following the forced administration of a major bank in 1994 and the collapse of others in 1995, a consolidation program was put in place to improve the condition of mostly small, weak, and undercapitalized banks, following largely unsuccessful earlier attempts on an individual bank basis. The program involved tougher supervision based on individual rescue plans and led to the discontinuation of the activities of many banks. Despite the central bank's extensive deposit guarantees (in addition to the deposit insurance scheme, mandatory since 1994), the public's trust in the banking system was shaken.

The government adopted a stabilization program for small banks in 1996 to improve banking system credibility. A state company purchased the nonperforming loans of the banks in the program at their face value, against the banks' obligation to write them off within seven years. The banks involved were subjected to a number of performance criteria in addition to general prudential rules. The program continued with varying success until 1999, leading to a consolidation of the small banking sector. The privatization program of major banks was put in place after 1997, improving the effectiveness and stability of the system.

Most of the bank failures in the process of banking system consolidation were attributed to fraud, credit risk, and bad management (corporate governance), and not to exposure to exchange rate risk. The limited link between exchange rate exposure and bank failures was mostly because banks with a significant FX exposure belonged to the better tier of institutions and foreign banks were very active in this market, having been allowed to operate either as subsidiaries or, more important, as branches of foreign institutions from the start. Permitting branches of foreign banks to operate in the domestic market also proved an important stabilizing element for the banking system, as well as during the FX crisis.

pegged regime period. The FX risk management was also helped by a gradual strengthening of prudential regulation and supervision during the 1990s, and by

the active involvement of foreign institutions and their branches. However, this gradual strengthening of the prudential and regulatory framework was not directly associated with the increased flexibility of the exchange rate. Although the CNB had kept limits on the open FX positions of banks from the early 1990s, other FX-risk-related prudential regulations came into effect only in 2000 in the context of EU harmonization rules that established capital adequacy rules for FX risks.

The FX market intervention strategy developed gradually in tandem with the exchange rate regime and alongside FX market development. Having been first used after the widening of the band in early 1996, interventions have become a standard policy tool since the exchange rate was floated in 1997. Interventions were used as a standard, though infrequent, tool to stabilize market fluctuations, including in response to large capital flows that could threaten the inflation target. Interventions have been based on limits and goals set by the Board, and implemented through major market players by operative decisions of the staff without a pre-determined system of allocation or bank rotation lists. The volumes of interventions have been published with a two-month lag since 1998, but no procedural rules exist as to whether the interventions are announced immediately; both practices have been used with varying success (Holub, 2005).

Challenges Faced during the Transition

One of the major challenges the authorities faced in exiting from the pegged regime was the difficulty in introducing an alternative monetary policy framework under near-crisis conditions. These conditions made it even more difficult to replace the exchange rate anchor with monetary targeting, while the conditions for a successful IT were not fully in place at the outset. With so little preparation time (six months), the authorities were caught unprepared for the challenges of the new framework under a floating exchange rate. The following were the main challenges:

- Public support and awareness: Owing to the lack of a communication strategy, there was very little public awareness about the new regime. This lack of awareness naturally had an adverse effect on the level of public support. Since late 1998, the CNB has been very active in communicating its strategy to the public and specific interest groups, which has proven to be beneficial in terms of gaining their support for the new regime (Jonas and Mishkin, 2003).

- The role of the government: The government was not involved in defining the new goal of price stability and setting inflation targets. The new regime essentially required a brand new interpretation of the law that until 2002 referred to currency stability. Given the lack of agreement with the government, the CNB chose CPI net of administered prices to target inflation, which raised communication and statistical problems in the subsequent period. Since

2000, the government has been involved in quantifying inflation targets and has assumed responsibility for supporting the IT regime.

- The CNB's internal processes: The CNB's internal processes were not adequately equipped for the information and technical requirements of monetary policymaking under IT. It had very little capacity to forecast inflation with reasonable precision and analyze other macroeconomic developments. The staff responsible for forecasting inflation focused their attention on information collection, rather than on their role of undertaking analyses for monetary policy decision making. The elements of a proper forecasting and policy analysis were put in place only by 2000 (Čapek and others, 2003b).

- The credibility of the new regime: The lack of some of these supporting elements of the IT framework indeed proved costly in terms of establishing the credibility of the new regime. The undershooting of the targets in the early years was associated with a protracted recession with rising unemployment, which endangered the independence of the CNB (see Jonas and Mishkin, 2003; and Čapek and others, 2003a).[12] Although the CNB's independence was preserved, these pressures underpinned the importance of achieving the consent of the key parties (the government and the public in particular) in setting the inflation trajectory.

Lessons from the Czech Experience

The following lessons can be derived from the Czech experience:

- The Czech experience underscores the importance of maintaining consistency between the peg regime and the mix of macroeconomic policies under relatively open capital accounts in avoiding disorderly exits from a pegged exchange rate regime. When policies are not in line with the peg, attempts to adjust the regime toward flexibility provide only a temporary relief and postpone an eventual adjustment.

- The authorities' efforts to strengthen the condition of the banking system and put in place reasonably well developed financial markets and instruments for risk management helped limit the severity of the disorderly exit and facilitated implementation of the new exchange rate regime and policy framework.

- The experience also underscores the importance of adequate preparation for IT, public and government

---

[12]Whether or not high real interest rates were kept unduly long was not clear ex ante, particularly because there was a need to preserve credibility in the face of rising inflation. With the benefit of hindsight, a proper forecasting system could perhaps have allowed an earlier relaxation of the policy (Čapek and others, 2003a).

The BCU adopted a new intervention strategy with the move to the floating regime and considerably increased the transparency of its FX operations immediately after the crisis. At the beginning of the free float period, interventions in the FX market were limited to fulfilling the BCU needs, established in advance. The objectives, amounts, and procedures of all BCU interventions were made explicit. Starting in November 2003, BCU purchases of foreign currency were performed through auctions announced at the beginning of the day. Transparency of the government's FX transactions did not increase, however, with the latter channelled in the market through the state bank.

Since 2005, monetary policy has become more transparent and interventions in the FX market have been carried out and perceived as an instrument to achieve monetary and inflationary goals. Indeed, the reputation gained by the BCU through its actions began to allow for a more flexible use of the instruments and auctions in the exchange market. Since September 2005, the BCU interventions have not been announced in advance, although they are reported ex post on the BCU's website.

Communication Strategies

High levels of transparency and communication of the monetary policy framework were also major goals of the monetary authorities after the move to a free float regime. In 2003, Monetary Policy Reports were issued quarterly and regular meetings with economic analysts helped explain the monetary authorities' assessment of inflationary trends, policy actions, and achievement of the monetary targets. Since January 2004, the monetary authorities have conducted surveys of inflation expectations and the results have been made publicly available. The objectives, amounts, and procedures of all BCU interventions in the FX market were made explicit until October 2005, to allow market participants to develop credible views on the exchange rate and future monetary policy. Since the BCU gained a strong reputation, interventions in the FX market have no longer been explicit.

The Financial Safety Net

A number of measures had been taken to strengthen the banking system in the late 1990s prior to the float, but they were not adequate to improve the capacity to assess and manage FX risks. In September 1998, the BCU increased the minimum capital adequacy requirements from 8 percent to 10 percent of risk-weighted assets to strengthen the resilience of the banking sector. However, because this increase was not currency specific, FX risk was not internalized and hence the regulatory framework and bank behavior continued to undervalue FX risk. Moreover, reserve requirements in foreign currency held at the BCU were remunerated

at above-market interest rates. The movement to a free float in a context of a high level of dollarization had raised concerns about banks' and the government's solvency, leading to an increase in the bank run.

After the movement to a free float regime, important changes in prudential regulation on FX risk have been adopted to strengthen the capacity to manage FX risks (2002–05): Liquidity requirements on foreign currency deposits have been raised, and reserve requirements in foreign currency started to be remunerated at below-market rates. Exposure to unhedged FX risk has been incorporated in loan classification and provisioning purposes (stress tests for large loans have been requested), and more information has been required for foreign-currency-denominated loans (including business plans and audited financial statements). Capital requirements have been made currency specific: risk weights on dollar loans to the nonfinancial private sector were set at 125 percent, and they have also been increased for foreign currency loans to the public sector. Moreover, capital requirements against market risk have been established. Finally, foreign currency deposits have been assigned a lower coverage and a higher risk premium has been charged by the Deposit Insurance Agency.

Lessons from the Uruguayan Experience

The following lessons can be drawn from the experience of Uruguay:

• The absence of the supporting elements to deal with greater flexibility and the misperception of FX risks in the context of high financial dollarization and fiscal weakness make an abrupt exit from a pegged regime very challenging. The challenges faced in stabilizing the economy during the crisis highlight the importance of early preparations in achieving a smooth transition to greater flexibility.

• In particular, the absence of a strong and sound financial system with appropriate prudential rules to manage exposure to FX flexibility, and the lack of markets and instruments to hedge FX risks, magnify the challenges of a crisis exit. Moreover, the absence of domestic monetary instruments robust to changes in the monetary regime limits the ability of the authorities to support an alternative monetary framework.

• Intensifying efforts to put in place the supporting elements of a flexible exchange rate regime can help minimize the period of uncertainty, thereby helping market participants cope with flexible rates. In particular, prompt establishment of an alternative monetary framework and the development of the capacity to implement it are essential in restoring monetary credibility under floating exchange rates.

- The adoption of consistent macroeconomic monetary policies, including on the fiscal side, also supports the steps taken to gradually increase monetary credibility and inflation control within a flexible exchange rate regime.

- The experience also emphasizes the importance of transparent and explicit communication of monetary, exchange rate, and intervention policies in rebuilding credibility following a sudden and disorderly exit.

Appendix I From Fixed to Float: Operational Ingredients of Durable Exits to Flexible Exchange Rates

This appendix summarizes the main points of the IMF's operational framework for moving toward flexibility for those countries that have decided to move to a more market-determined exchange rate.[1] This framework provides hands-on guidance on the institutional, operational, and technical aspects of moving toward exchange rate flexibility, drawing on the experience of countries that have managed the transition.

Operational Ingredients of Durable Exits from Fixed to Floating Regimes

Although the timing and priority accorded to each of these areas may vary from country to country depending on initial conditions and economic structure, the successful ingredients for floating include:[2]

- Developing a *deep and liquid foreign exchange (FX) market*;

- Formulating *intervention policies* consistent with the new exchange rate regime;

- Establishing an *alternative nominal anchor* in the context of a new monetary policy framework and developing supportive markets; and

- Reviewing exchange rate exposures and building the capacity of market participants, including the public sector, to *manage exchange rate risks* and of the supervisory authorities to regulate and monitor them.

Developing a Deep and Liquid FX Market

Operating a flexible exchange rate regime works well only when there is a sufficiently liquid and efficient FX market for price discovery.[3] A well-functioning FX market allows the exchange rate to respond to market forces and helps to minimize instances and durations of disruptive day-to-day fluctuations in the exchange rate and longer-term deviations from equilibrium. Fixing the exchange rate itself is often a key factor in limiting FX market liquidity. A central bank operating a fixed exchange rate regime is usually active in the market by necessity, which reduces the need for market participants to trade and keeps them from gaining experience in price formation or exchange rate risk management. In the extreme, the central bank may dominate the interbank FX market and act as the primary FX intermediary.

Allowing some exchange rate flexibility is a key step that can help improve the depth and efficiency of the FX market and stimulate better risk management. Such flexibility, in turn, could limit what is, to some extent, an unavoidable chicken-and-egg problem: Exchange rate flexibility requires a deep market and better risk management, but a deep market and prudent risk management require flexibility. Fluctuations in the exchange rate, even if small, quickly create incentives for market participants to gather information, form views, price foreign exchange, and manage exchange rate risks. Creating a sense of two-way risk in the exchange rate is also essential in establishing a deep market and capacity to manage risks. Market perceptions that the exchange rate can either appreciate or depreciate help reduce the risk of one-way bets against the central bank, minimize

---

[1]This summary, prepared by Neil Saker, draws on IMF (2004a and 2004b), which in turn draws heavily on Duttagupta, Fernandez, and Karacadag (2004).

[2]These are in addition to the role of sound macroeconomic and structural policies—including fiscal discipline, monetary policy credibility, and a sound financial sector—which are essential to maintaining any type of regime, fixed or floating.

[3]The FX market in general consists of a wholesale interbank market, in which authorized dealers (usually banks and other financial institutions) trade among themselves, and a retail market, in which authorized dealers transact with final customers (usually households and firms). The interbank market is where price discovery occurs through a decentralized allocation of FX by market participants on their own behalf as well as on behalf of their customers. A liquid market is characterized by (1) relatively narrow bid-offer spreads to lower transaction costs (tightness); (2) high turnover in volume as well as an abundance of orders to minimize the price impact of individual trades (depth and breadth); (3) efficient trading, clearing, and settlement systems to facilitate the swift execution of orders (immediacy); and (4) a wide range of active market participants to ensure that new orders flow quickly to correct order imbalances and misalignments (resiliency) (see Sarr and Lybek, 2002).

destabilizing trading strategies, and help foster better risk management expertise.

There are four key aspects of deepening the market and enhancing price discovery: (1) reducing the central bank's market-making role, including its quotation of buying and selling rates, and requiring market makers to provide two-way price quotations; (2) increasing market information and transparency on the sources and uses of foreign exchange, detailed economic data, and a coherent policy framework as a basis for market participants to develop accurate views on monetary and exchange rate policy and efficiently price foreign exchange; (3) eliminating (or phasing out) regulations that stifle market activity;[4] and (4) improving the market's microstructure, including by reducing market segmentation, improving the effectiveness of market intermediaries, and securing reliable and efficient settlement systems.

A Coherent FX Intervention Strategy

FX market intervention becomes discretionary under a flexible exchange rate regime, making it essential to establish well-specified intervention principles to enhance credibility of the new regime. The authorities face some difficult dilemmas and need to consider a number of important issues in this process:

- Potential disconnect between the exchange rate and macroeconomic fundamentals can create a role for intervention under floating exchange rates, even in well-functioning FX markets. But misalignments are difficult to detect and the typical indicators may not always allow policymakers to identify the degree of misalignment precisely enough to pinpoint appropriate intervention amounts and timing.[5]

- Volatility reflecting market illiquidity may warrant intervention, because the latter stifles trading and, if it persists, can have serious adverse effects. Intervention can jump-start the market or tip a perverse price trend in the other direction. However, short-term volatility may not always warrant intervention, especially when it occurs in an orderly

(liquid) market. Volatility often reflects the process of price discovery and provides useful signals to policymakers and the market. Efforts to smooth such volatility often end up suppressing useful signals and reduce incentives to learn how to manage FX risks.

- Exercising restraint in intervention during the transition to a flexible regime can help signal the official commitment to a market-determined exchange rate. Interventions that target an exchange rate level or a path can undermine the credibility of the new regime. By entering the market infrequently, central banks can maximize the element of surprise and the chances of intervention effectiveness and can build market confidence in the commitment to flexibility. As confidence grows, policy pronouncements and the capacity to intervene may suffice in most instances to achieve the desired change in the price trend, without an actual intervention operation.

- Even in fully flexible exchange rate regimes, central banks cannot completely avoid regular interventions (for example, to have a regular FX supply from purchases of the foreign currency revenue of public sector companies or export boards, or to target an appropriate level of reserves). Such interventions can be regular, preannounced, and rule-based (for example, through auctions) to support the information flow to the market, reduce noise, and enhance the signaling of surprise interventions.

The transition to flexible exchange rates hence creates the need to develop a coherent intervention strategy that specifies the policies on objectives, timing, and amounts of intervention. Whether the objective of intervention is to correct misalignments, calm disorderly market conditions, accumulate reserves, or supply publicly acquired foreign exchange to the market, care needs to be taken to signal the commitment to a market-determined rate and avoid excessive smoothing of short-term fluctuations. The latter is necessary to avoid suppressing the nascent markets and the useful market signals, as well as to avoid sending confusing messages about policy intentions. Intervention policy transparency is important in building confidence in the new regime, especially following forced exits. A public commitment to both the objectives of intervention and the criteria applied in its conduct enables market scrutiny and accountability for the central bank's FX operations.

Developing an Alternative Nominal Anchor under a New Monetary Policy Framework

Moving away from a fixed exchange rate creates the need to replace it with another credible nominal anchor and to redesign the monetary policy framework around the new anchor. The two tasks, in turn, require a substan-

---

[4]These regulations include, for example, (1) abolishing surrender requirements for FX receipts to the central bank, taxes and surcharges on FX transactions, restrictions on interbank trading (for example, outright bans on interbank trading or a requirement that all spot and forward market trades with customers have an underlying commercial transaction), and limits on price ranges quoted by dealers; (2) unifying segmented FX markets; and (3) relaxing current and, to some extent, capital account restrictions to bolster the sources and uses of foreign exchange in the market.

[5]These indicators include, for example, the nominal and real effective exchange rates, productivity and other competitiveness measures, the terms of trade, the current external account and balance of payments outlook, interest rate differentials, and parallel market exchange rates.

tial amount of capacity building and credibility building, and thus planning ahead for the transition is critical to achieving an orderly exit. The viability of maintaining a flexible regime without a nominal anchor depends on the authorities' credibility to sustain a responsible monetary policy without an anchor. Such credibility is generally difficult to build quickly, especially if a country had relied on a rigid exchange rate until the exit. Many countries moving to flexibility in recent years have favored IT frameworks over money-targeting ones (IMF, 2000a; and Khan, 2003). Although the latter can serve as a nominal anchor after floating, the weak relationship between monetary aggregates and inflation limits the effectiveness of such targets.

However, a credible alternative such as IT requires extensive preparation. A lengthy transition period reflects, in part, the time required to fulfill the necessary institutional requirements and macroeconomic conditions including (1) a central bank mandate to pursue an explicit, publicly announced inflation target as the overriding objective of monetary policy; (2) central bank operational independence; (3) transparency and accountability in the conduct and evaluation of monetary policy actions; (4) a reliable methodology for forecasting inflation and its link with other macroeconomic aggregates; (5) a forward-looking operating procedure that systematically incorporates forecasts into policy actions and responds to deviations from targets; (6) lack of fiscal dominance; and (7) a well-regulated and supervised financial sector (see Carare and others, 2002; Eichengreen and others, 1999; Fraga, Goldfajn, and Minella, 2003; IMF, 2000a and 2000b; and Mishkin, 2000).

The difficulty of developing a credible alternative nominal anchor to the exchange rate has also caused many countries to relinquish its anchor role only gradually or follow various versions of the monetary-targeting approach. Especially in the case of disorderly exits, some countries adopted monetary targets (namely, targeting base money, broad monetary aggregates, or bank reserves) in an effort to quickly establish a new nominal anchor and restore policy credibility until the preconditions of IT were established. Some countries used crawling bands as an intermediate regime for transitioning to another nominal anchor over a long period. The band usually has been set symmetrically around a crawling central parity and gradually widened over time as the tension between the exchange rate and the inflation rate objectives was eventually resolved in favor of the latter.

Capacity to Assess and Manage FX Risks

Private sector FX risk exposures can have an important bearing on the pace of exit, the type of flexible exchange rate regime adopted, and official intervention policies. Floating the exchange rate moves exchange rate exposure from the public to private sector balance sheets, as central banks no longer stand ready to intervene at fixed rates (Allen and others, 2002).[6] Determining the scale and scope of FX risk exposures in the financial and nonfinancial sectors is therefore a key area for countries planning an orderly exit from pegs. Early analysis of, and improvements in, the management of FX risk are particularly important in economies where dollarization and currency mismatches are high. Even when these risks are modest early on, market participants need to develop the capacity to measure and monitor them to avoid building up exposures over time.

Evaluating exchange rate risk exposures involves detailed balance sheet analysis—focusing on the currency composition of balance sheets and the maturity, liquidity, and quality of foreign currency assets and liabilities. Unhedged FX borrowing by the corporate sector can translate into massive losses for banks and a surge in demand for foreign currency. Banks often closely control foreign currency liabilities and assets, but even when these are matched, the use of short-term foreign currency funds to finance long-term FX loans to unhedged borrowers causes their FX risks to translate into sizable credit and liquidity risks for banks (indirect FX risks). Two related risks also require close attention: (1) maturity mismatches in banks' foreign currency books that expose them to foreign currency liquidity risks and (2) corporate and banking sector exposure to interest rate risk that can limit the extent to which the central bank can use interest rates instead of interventions in the FX market. Corporations in developing countries have particular difficulty off-loading interest rate risk, particularly because they may not be able to obtain long-term fixed rates for their liabilities to fund assets.

An orderly exit from a pegged regime hence requires close scrutiny of the private sector's capacity to manage FX risk. Market participants need to develop information systems monitoring the FX risks, analytical systems for risk measurement, and internal risk and prudential procedures. Adequate prudential and supervisory arrangements need to complement internal risk management systems. Prudential measures may include limits on net open positions (as a percentage of capital), foreign currency lending (as a percentage of foreign currency liabilities), and overseas borrowing and bond issuance (as a percentage of capital); limits on the range of FX operations banks are allowed to perform; capital requirements against FX lending or risk;[7] and the

---

[6]The public sector remains exposed to risks relating to its foreign-currency-denominated public debt.

[7]The Basel Committee recommends a capital charge of 8 percent on the open position based on the shorthand method and recommends that the net open position does not exceed 2 percent of capital, although countries with greater risk exposures may need to adopt more conservative limits (Basel Committee on Banking Supervision, 1996). All open position calculations should include net spot and forward positions, guarantees, and net future income and expenses not yet accrued, but already fully hedged.

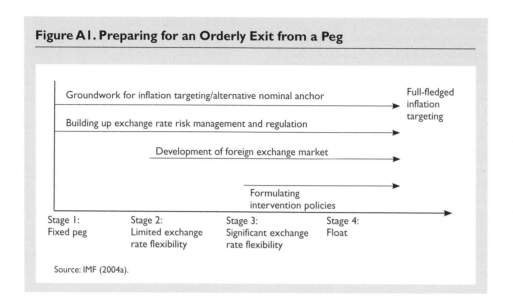

Figure A1. Preparing for an Orderly Exit from a Peg

Groundwork for inflation targeting/alternative nominal anchor

Full-fledged inflation targeting

Building up exchange rate risk management and regulation

Development of foreign exchange market

Formulating intervention policies

Stage 1: Fixed peg

Stage 2: Limited exchange rate flexibility

Stage 3: Significant exchange rate flexibility

Stage 4: Float

Source: IMF (2004a).

issuance of regulations or guidelines on the design of banks' internal control systems. Improving the capacity to enforce regulations can help ensure that regulations are complied with and are effective. Developing a risk-based supervisory system can help ensure that the internal control systems are adequate and properly enforced.

Although early investment into these elements is typically beneficial on its own, it can also help in mitigating the risk of disorderly exits during market turbulences. For instance, providing for a two-way risk when developing FX markets reduces the scope for destabilizing risk strategies. Similarly, having an effective FX-risk-related supervisory and prudential framework can prevent contagion of financial crises.

Carefully developed derivatives markets for foreign exchange are an essential element in building capacity to manage FX risks. However, facilitating the development of risk-hedging instruments by lifting controls on forward market activity can be a double-edged sword. While improving risk management capacity and supporting FX market development, liberalization of forward transactions could also facilitate speculative activity where there are incentives to do so. Several considerations can help guide the safe use of derivatives. Such instruments require financial institutions (and corporations) that have achieved a certain level of sophistication in risk management and supervisory authorities capable of conducting risk-based supervision. Close monitoring of the use of the instruments is important to prevent their being used to push a normally sustainable situation over the edge by sizable leveraged bets. Also critical are the standardization of derivative products traded among banks and the presence of accounting standards for fair valuation and a reliable

legal system for contract enforcement. The central bank should promote market transparency and, with other regulators, promote high reporting standards.

Pace and Sequencing of Exit to Exchange Rate Flexibility

There are important policy questions regarding the pace of exit and sequencing of moves toward exchange rate flexibility with other policies, including capital account liberalization. These questions involve difficult trade-offs and considerations that are often country-specific, including the degree of preparedness for floating rates, the openness of the capital account, the macroeconomic situation, and the condition in the domestic and international markets. Some broad conclusions are as follows:

- If taken from a position of macroeconomic strength, a faster pace of exit has benefits in that it signals purpose and determination, thereby enhancing the credibility of monetary policy. It also has a greater chance of exploiting what may turn out to be a narrow window of tranquility, provided also that the institutional underpinnings for operating a floating exchange rate are in place.

- In practice, the pace at which relevant institutions (for example, an alternative nominal anchor and the capacity to manage risks) can be built is a main determinant of the pace at which an orderly exit can proceed. Many countries have opted for a gradual approach, which in principle may reduce the risk of excessive exchange rate volatility and its potentially adverse effects on inflationary expectations. It also allows the FX market to deepen through the mutually reinforcing relationship between FX activity and exchange rate flexibility and provides time to build the remaining institutional blocks.

- Early preparation for an exchange rate float can bolster the chances of success of the exit strategy—gradual or rapid. Many of the operational areas require substantial information on the exposures to and capacity to manage FX risk, and increasing data on balance of payments developments. These steps can be undertaken early on, even before a peg is exited. The second stage may involve allowing some exchange rate flexibility to stimulate FX market activity and continuing to develop other operational areas. Intervention policies can be addressed at a relatively later stage, once greater exchange rate flexibility is embraced (see Appendix Figure A1 for a suggestive illustration of the various stages taken toward moving to full flexibility).

- The absence of a full-fledged IT framework as an alternative nominal anchor should not preclude a rapid exit strategy, provided that there is a robust commitment to price stability. The building blocks of IT—such as fiscal discipline, operational independence of the monetary authorities to pursue low inflation, and transparency and accountability—are necessary for the success of any monetary policy regime regardless of a formal adoption of IT.

- The pace of exit also needs to take into account the openness of the capital account. For example, it may be difficult to pursue a gradual exit strategy under conditions characterized by large and volatile capital flows. By contrast, a less open capital account would make it easier to operate variants of pegs or manage the exchange rate within a band. Clear trade-offs are involved in the sequencing of exchange rate flexibility and capital account liberalization.[8]

- There are risks to opening the capital account before adopting a flexible exchange rate; many countries were forced off pegs after sudden reversals of capital flows, whereas others faced heavy inflows and appreciation pressures and had to allow flexibility to avoid overheating. On the other hand, liberalizing the capital account can help offset transitory current account shocks, expand the instruments for risk management, and deepen the FX market, which is important for operating a flexible exchange rate.

- The transition to flexibility can be facilitated by removing or strengthening existing asymmetries in the openness of the capital account to support an orderly correction of misalignments (for example, by liberalizing outflows to reduce pressures from inflows, and liberalizing long-term inflows before short-term ones). Remaining controls can be removed following a successful move to floating.

---

[8]The successful liberalization of the capital account itself depends on a wide range of issues related to the economy, financial sector stability and reform, and sequencing issues (see Ishii and others, 2002).

Appendix II Experiences with Short-Lived Exits to Greater Flexibility[1]

The experiences of the countries presented below highlight a number of factors relating to macro conditions, commitment to reform, and operational aspects that have contributed to reversals in the attempts to establish greater exchange rate flexibility. In particular, they highlight the roles of (1) an underdeveloped and illiquid FX market (Uzbekistan), (2) a limited capacity to manage exchange rate risk with ensuing fear of floating (all three cases), (3) a lack of an appropriate (for example, rules-based) intervention policy (Uzbekistan and Pakistan), (4) a limited institutional and technical capacity to adopt a credible alternative nominal anchor (Uzbekistan and Pakistan), (5) a limited degree of monetary policy independence (Ecuador and Uzbekistan), (6) adverse economic conditions and poor macroeconomic policy (Ecuador), and (7) a lack of commitment to free (exchange) markets (Pakistan and Uzbekistan).

Ecuador

In February 1999, the Ecuadorian authorities abandoned the exchange rate band and moved to a floating exchange rate regime after repeated episodes of exchange market pressures. The Ecuadorian economy plunged into a major economic crisis in 1999: Real GDP declined by about 7.5 percent; inflation accelerated to 61 percent; the fiscal deficit exceeded 5 percent of GDP; public debt grew to over 100 percent of GDP and was in default; unemployment almost doubled to 17 percent; FX reserves fell by 64 percent; and volatility of the sucre continued well after the floating, depreciating by 200 percent in 1999.

Simultaneously Ecuador was hit by a major crisis in the banking sector. The crisis originated in persistent institutional weaknesses in banking supervision and regulation that allowed excessive accumulation of credit risk from connected and foreign currency lending to unhedged borrowers. The weaknesses in the banking system were exacerbated by a tradition of bailing out troubled banks. Lack of effective supervi-

sion of offshore subsidiaries of banks provided an easy way to circumvent regulations and controls and ultimately contributed substantially to the losses of failed banks.

The banking crisis further weakened monetary and exchange rate policy, which resulted in renewed exchange market pressure at the end of 1999. With shattered monetary policy credibility, looming hyperinflation, and no access to international financial markets after the sovereign default on the Brady bonds in the fall of 1999, the authorities moved to a full-blown dollarization in January 2000.

Pakistan

Pakistan made two attempts to introduce greater exchange rate flexibility from a de facto peg to the U.S. dollar. The first move took place during 1998, when a number of liberalization measures were undertaken (based on the recommendations of an IMF mission in 1997) to allow greater scope for market determination of the exchange rate. The process was interrupted in May and June 1998 with the introduction of exchange controls and a dual exchange system. In May 1999 the exchange rate system was unified and an initial attempt was made at liberalizing the exchange rate by allowing authorized dealers to quote their own buying and selling rates.

However, the authorities reversed some of the liberalization measures. Only a month later, they imposed a narrow exchange rate band. In May 2000, they made a new attempt at liberalizing the exchange rate and invited an IMF mission to advise on a framework for money and FX market operations. However, the authorities continued their strong preference for maintaining nominal exchange rate stability through (1) direct and indirect interventions on the official and parallel markets, (2) exertion of moral suasion on market participants, (3) close monitoring of bank's activity, (4) imposition of restrictions on authorized dealers' FX operations, and (5) other indirect forms of intervention (for example, managing import demand). All these restrictive measures hampered the interplay of demand and supply in the FX market and did not allow an

---

[1]Prepared by Jahanara Zaman.

exchange rate adjustment as warranted by the underlying macroeconomic conditions.

Pakistan's slow progress toward greater flexibility suggests a lack of operational preparedness. The FX market is not sufficiently liquid; the intervention policy has not been developed to yield consistent and transparent outcomes; formal adoption of IT is still in process; and the institutional capacity to manage exchange rate risk is not fully developed.

Uzbekistan

In July 2001, the authorities took steps toward greater exchange rate flexibility motivated primarily by a consideration to implement economic reforms. An over-the-counter market was created for buying and selling foreign exchange to allow the exchange rate to float freely in accordance with demand and supply, but the market remained shallow. Progress toward a market economy was slowing because of excessive government control, including (1) restrictions on domestic and external trade, (2) numerous barriers to the normal functioning of the financial markets, and (3) exchange restrictions and controls (including surrender requirements and restrictions on interbank sales of foreign exchange).

The financial sector remained weak with substantial vulnerabilities related to FX risk. Uzbekistan's banking system was characterized by extensive government controls and limited confidence in financial intermediation. In addition, banks had large exposures to FX risk. Uzbek banks were heavily dependent on foreign financing, and a reduction in the flows of such financing would jeopardize their ability to continue to finance the domestic economy.

A fear of floating led to frequent intervention in the FX market and to a reversal to a more tightly managed exchange rate regime. The fear of floating stemmed from a number of factors, including a strong pass-through from the exchange rate to inflation, the potential impact of the high level of liability dollarization on private sector balance sheets, potential output costs of variable exchange rates, and concerns about the implications for the heavy dependence of Uzbek banks on external borrowing.

Appendix III Ukraine: An Example of Ongoing Cautious Steps toward Greater Exchange Rate Flexibility[1]

Ukraine's move toward exchange rate flexibility is motivated by the difficulties in maintaining a fixed exchange rate with an increasingly more open capital account and a surge in foreign exchange receipts from the large current account surplus. Since 1999 the authorities have maintained a de facto peg to the U.S. dollar, but over time the balance of payments situation has changed from being at the brink of default to a sizable current account surplus (though more recently, the current account balance switched from a large surplus to a deficit). Short-term capital inflows attracted by the perception of exchange rate undervaluation added to the pressure on the hryvnia in 2005 and complicated the control over monetary aggregates and inflation.

In response to these developments, the authorities took a number of actions in 2005. They increased sterilization operations and prohibited nonresident purchases of short-term treasury bills. They have also taken some initial steps to increase exchange rate flexibility by allowing a step appreciation of the hryvnia and introducing an indicative narrow band of HRV1/US$5.0–$5.2; the official exchange rate has been left unchanged at HRV1/US$5.05, however, and the interbank market rate has mostly moved in a narrower band of HRV1/US$5.00–$5.06. Furthermore, since late 2004 the authorities have been focusing on preparations for the introduction of an IT regime as an alternative nominal anchor.

The authorities' approach to moving toward greater exchange rate flexibility has been very cautious, reflecting a number of challenges typically associated with fear of floating: concerns about losing a transparent nominal anchor and policy credibility, potential exchange rate losses associated with currency mismatches in corporate balance sheets, weaknesses in banks' risk management practices and lack of hedging markets and instruments to cover against exchange rate risks, underdeveloped financial markets, and fears of worsening of external competitiveness should the currency appreciate.

Some progress has been made in most of the areas identified in the fixed-to-float framework and technical assistance (TA) reviews, but further efforts are needed.[2] First, with a view to establishing the elements of an inflation-targeting framework, the National Bank of Ukraine (NBU) has started improving its modeling and forecasting capacity over the past two years, communicating more on the introduction of IT, and improving monetary policy transparency. Further efforts are needed to firmly establish NBU's operational independence, clarify the primacy of price stability as the main monetary policy objective, continue efforts to strengthen the communication strategy, and deepen financial markets and instruments. The efforts to accelerate the preparations have been undermined by an uncertain political environment.

Second, the spot and forward foreign exchange markets remain substantially underdeveloped and illiquid. A high degree of regulation and dominant central bank presence in the market have been key obstacles to market development. To address these issues, the NBU undertook measures in 2005 to relax restrictions on forward transactions, on open foreign exchange positions, and on banks' two-way trading and to make foreign exchange trading more flexible and transparent. These measures have not yet become productive, reflecting in part the existence of a fee on foreign exchange transactions and the absence of liquid interbank and government securities markets to facilitate price formation in the forward market.

Third, banks and borrowers continue to remain vulnerable to foreign exchange and related risks. Existing limits on short positions seem to be binding, but in practice the banks tend to balance their foreign exchange liabilities with foreign exchange credits, extending them even to

---

[1]Prepared by Inci Ötker-Robe and David Vávra.

[2]To support the transition, the authorities have received extensive technical assistance from the IMF since late 2004 in the areas of moving to greater exchange rate flexibility; monetary operations; monetary policy communication; bank supervision, regulation, and resolution; development of the government securities market; and establishing the remaining conditions conducive to adopting an IT regime that could replace the exchange rate anchor.

clients with no foreign currency earnings; foreign-currency-denominated lending has been about 40 percent of total loans since 2001 and has edged up recently to over 40 percent. The NBU tightened supervision and regulation of banks, and introduced higher provisioning requirements for foreign exchange lending to unhedged borrowers to address indirect foreign exchange risks. However, banks also face maturity risks, with maturities of bank funding not having kept up with the increase in loan maturities. A potential funding risk for banks also emerged, because the rising dollarization of loans has required banks to borrow foreign funds, making banks vulnerable to rollover and liquidity risks.

Finally, lack of adequate capacity to affect market interest rates hinders the introduction of IT as well as the capacity to implement a flexible exchange rate regime. Although the central bank has several instruments to steer market liquidity, it lacks a transparent policy rate to influence short-term interest rates. The discount rate, the NBU's policy rate, has no influence on interest rates, and the refinancing rate has lost its signaling function. Reserve requirements have played an increasingly large role in steering liquidity, not least because of lower fiscal costs compared with other sterilization instruments, but have caused significant interest rate volatility, raised spreads between borrowing and lending rates, and led to concerns about their implications for financial intermediation. The NBU has recently increased its focus in this area to improve the functioning of its monetary instruments.

Appendix IV Foreign Exchange Hedging, Complementary Markets, and the Role of the Central Bank[1]

Foreign exchange risk is present in any modern economy. The risks may not be recognized or transparent, they might be ignored or implicitly transferred or assumed by official entities, or they may be measured and managed. Financial theory as well as extensive experience strongly suggests that failure to explicitly measure and manage risk by the entities that create that risk is potentially destabilizing, at both the institutional and systemic levels. Moreover, FX markets are only one of many financial system components, which are becoming increasingly integrated in developed economies. For reasons of appropriate risk management as well as efficient functioning of the financial system, development of the FX markets requires well-developed hedging and complementary markets.

Hedging

Open or unhedged FX exposures pose significant risks and can cause significant losses or even insolvency. The losses can often spread beyond those directly affected to their creditors, especially financial intermediaries, including commercial banks. If severe and widespread, the losses can pose systemic risks to the financial system.

Hedging FX exposures obviously reduces risk to the individual institution, but also has several other important benefits. It makes risks explicit, which allows them to be better measured, priced, and managed. It also allows the trading and transfer of risk, presumably to those better able to manage it. This improved allocation of risk in the economy should improve overall stability and yield important welfare benefits.

The central bank can play a key role in stimulating FX hedging. It can make clear the need for hedging; it can help assure that the means of hedging are available; and it can promote the effectiveness of hedging and reduce its cost. The central bank should ensure that the

environment and conditions permit and are supportive of hedging; it can also assume an active role in promoting the development of hedging.

Establishing the need for hedging is best done by making FX risks transparent and making it clear who bears them. Every effort should be made to avoid the creation or appearance of a moral hazard issue, whereby the creators of risk assume that the cost will be borne by others. Specifically, the central bank should eliminate explicit or implicit guarantees, multiple exchange rates, and subsidies. Suppressing volatility of the exchange rate, smoothing operations, or providing a predetermined path of the exchange rate all inhibit management of FX risk, especially when combined with interest rate differentials that are not consistent with the predetermined level or range of the exchange rate. Increased variability of the exchange rate will provide an incentive for hedging practices. The central bank should promote the use of market exchange rates for all transactions, transfer commercial transactions to the market, and reduce the factors that create segmentation among market participants.

Prudential regulations and supervision should recognize the benefits of financial hedging. Business plans should explicitly address FX exposures, and lenders and financial intermediaries should examine their client's risk management policies and procedures. Where appropriate, specific regulation might be called for, including higher provisioning requirements on FX loans to borrowers with no FX income, or higher capital requirements against unhedged FX exposures.

The central bank has an important role in making available the means to hedge FX risks: It should eliminate unnecessary regulatory obstacles that stifle market development. These include surrender requirements, restrictions on instruments such as forwards and options, and restrictions on market participants. For example, restrictions on types of transactions (for example, short selling), or parties to certain transactions (for example, nonresidents prevented from engaging in certain transactions), hinder the development of the market and can introduce serious distortions. The legal framework

---

[1]Prepared by Barry Topf.

should be modernized and adapted for modern financial markets, tax issues that increase the cost of hedging should be addressed, and tax discrimination should be eliminated. Accounting standards should provide for appropriate treatment of hedging transactions.

The central bank can undertake efforts to increase awareness and hedging skills in the relevant sectors of the public, including users as well as third parties, such as accountants and auditors. It can support professional groups (ACI)[2] and the setting of standards (CFA),[3] as well as market codes of conduct; it can also support the adoption of master agreements and standard documentation of transactions (ISDA[4]). It could also consider providing support to the market by making available objective benchmarks and pricing mechanisms, such as FX and interest rate fixings. In this case the central bank should play a statistical role only, leaving the market to actually determine the rates.

Foreign entities can often bring valuable experience and skills in risk management and should be allowed to play a constructive role. Other financial intermediaries, such as nonbank market makers and brokers, can also contribute to market development.

The effectiveness of hedging depends primarily on the efficiency of the markets and instruments, and the skills of those employing it. Nevertheless, the central bank can also play a useful role. An efficient infrastructure is vital, and payment and clearing systems should meet accepted standards. Safe and efficient payment versus payment and delivery versus payment are essential to a well-functioning financial system, as is the availability of reliable financial data and information. Even where the central bank is not the regulatory authority, a degree of market surveillance can be extremely helpful, especially in the early stages of market development.

Complementary Financial Markets

The FX market cannot develop independently of other financial markets. In a modern financial system, markets are highly integrated, information and capital flow quickly, and segmentation is costly and difficult to maintain. Lack of development in one market can retard the development of other markets, introduce inefficiencies and distortions, and hold back positive developments in the economy. Well-developed markets, on the other hand, reinforce one another, promote effi-

ciency, and spur continued development. FX markets are especially dependent on other markets, because FX transactions rarely stand alone: They are often derived from or connected to the need to transact or manage risk in other markets.

Short-term money markets have the closest link to FX markets because the most basic FX transactions are no more than transfers of bank balances. FX and money market transactions often complement one another, and in some cases can be substitutes. Furthermore, the interest rates established in the money market are vital for developing the FX market, especially that for forward and swap transactions, important hedging tools. A liquid and efficient interbank market in loans and deposits is essential to allow interest rate parity to function.

Within the FX market itself, foreign exchange versus foreign exchange transactions are important risk management tools (in addition to the FX versus domestic currency transactions that local players will naturally concentrate on). Derivative markets are important adjuncts to the FX market. Forward and swap transactions usually develop in close conjunction with the (spot) FX market and money market, whereas long-dated swaps, futures, and options usually come later.

Fixed-income markets, especially the government bond market, also play key roles. A liquid government bond market, in addition to its important role in government finance and monetary operations, provides a benchmark to other markets. Absence of a well-developed liquid securities market undermines the market's ability to price swaps, forwards, and other hedging instruments. A developed capital market complements banking markets, broadens the universe of available assets, diversifies financing channels, and improves operational efficiency.

The role of the central bank in promoting the development of complementary markets is analogous to its role in developing the hedging market. It can eliminate unnecessary obstacles, such as restrictions on instruments or techniques (such as short sales), and reduce excessive licensing, reporting, or regulatory burdens that stifle market development. It should help establish a strong bank supervisory capability—usually involving coordination with other authorities, including capital market regulators, securities regulators, and organized exchanges—and supervisory authorities of nonbank financial institutions.

Although it may not be its direct responsibility, the central bank can assist in establishing a conducive environment for market development. The bank can do this by reducing or eliminating institutional segmentation (by product or by customer), clarifying and rationalizing legal issues (such as treatment of collateral and repurchase (repo) transactions), promoting an efficient and transparent tax regime, and eliminating tax discrimination. Clear and modern accounting and reporting standards are also essential. The central bank could also play a supporting role in establishing efficient mar-

---

[2]ACI, the Financial Markets Association, has branches in many countries; it undertakes training activities and promotes best market practices.

[3]The CFA (Certified Financial Analyst) charter is granted by the Certified Financial Analyst Institute.

[4]The International Swap Dealers Association promotes standard documentation for financial transactions.

Box A1. The Bank of Israel's Role in Developing Foreign Exchange and Complementary Markets

The Bank of Israel (BoI) has twice played a direct role in developing markets by issuing derivative financial instruments for the sole purpose of kick-starting financial markets in new instruments. The outcomes were very different, but both illustrate important points.

The first attempt involved the use of foreign exchange options. All sectors of the economy had extensive experience—not always successful—in dealing with foreign exchange risk. As a result, the use of swaps and forwards, but not options, developed on its own. Moreover, although hedging was widespread in dealing with foreign exchange and foreign exchange exposures, hedging was not widely practiced in dealing with fluctuations of the domestic currency (the new Israeli sheqel—NIS). In part, lack of this sort of hedging stemmed from a long history of managed exchange rates. Managed exchange rates led to a perception that exchange rate risk was a matter for the authorities—the central bank and government—rather than market participants. Available hedging instruments were lacking, and there were indications that this situation stemmed more from lack of supply than lack of demand. Early in 1989, Israel adopted a horizontal band, allowing limited foreign exchange rate flexibility (±3 percent), which replaced the previous regime of a fixed peg with periodic—and not infrequent—devaluations (see Section III).

In 1989 the BoI began selling call options on the U.S. dollar by means of auctions to the commercial banks. (Because of legal restrictions, the central bank could not deal directly with the public or business sector, and the restriction of operating exclusively through commercial banks was itself seen as a considerable disadvantage.) The BoI wanted its involvement in call options to serve as a catalyst to developing the market, and therefore carefully limited its role so as to avoid substituting for private sector activity. The amount issued was set at $24 million per week, and never increased. Although the total amount issued was capped at $24 million per week, changes were made in issuance policy: put options and six-month maturities, in addition to the original three-month contracts, were added.

The market developed steadily thereafter. An over-the-counter (OTC) market began in 1990, and in 1994 the Tel Aviv Stock Exchange began trading options contracts (in 2002 it added NIS/euro contracts). In 1996, volume in both the OTC and the Stock Exchange began increasing rapidly. Because the amounts issued by the BoI remained the same, their share in the market shrank steadily: By 2004, BoI options accounted for less than 3 percent of outstanding options and less than 0.5 percent of turnover. In 2005, the

BoI ceased issuing three-month foreign exchange options, but continued issuing six-month contracts. By that time, the market was well established and stopping the issuance of these products had no noticeable effect on options trading.

The active role played by the BoI undoubtedly acted as a catalyst, at least partially, in developing the foreign exchange options market. Although the claim can be made—quite rightly—that such a market would have developed on its own, the initiative of the central bank certainly accelerated its appearance, and quite probably made the process more efficient. In addition, the BoI options provided an important source of data and information on exchange rate developments and expectations.

The BoI had less success in promoting the use of interest rate hedging instruments. Interest rate exposure was less recognized and hardly managed at all. This situation was the result of a history of high inflation, widespread indexation of financial assets and liabilities, a fragmented market, and extensive government interference. By 1990, the focus of the BoI's monetary policy shifted to interest rates. In that year, the BoI began to auction three-month future contacts based on 3- and 12-month treasury bills, in an effort to spur the practice of interest rate hedging.

Interest rate risk hedging markets developed much more slowly than did those for foreign exchange risk, and have remained fairly small and illiquid. OTC trading of interest rate forwards developed sporadically, and exchange traded contracts were introduced only in 2000, and discontinued shortly thereafter owing to low trading volumes. In 2004, total outstanding OTC interest rate derivatives reached NIS 4 billion, compared with NIS 160 billion for foreign exchange derivatives. This ratio differs substantially from international experience, where interest rate derivatives comprise 80 percent of outstanding derivatives positions, far greater than the 14 percent share of foreign exchange derivatives.

The lack of development of interest rate hedging remains a puzzle, but a number of factors can be cited. Historically, risk was managed through consumer price indexation and real interest rate denominated contracts, rather than nominal interest rate instruments. There has been a shorter history of interest rate volatility, and government debt issuance policy has not always been helpful. The underlying market is illiquid, fragmented, and incomplete and there are still administrative obstacles—no short selling or security lending and no market makers (although there are plans for government bond market makers to begin operations in 2006). The lack of clear enforceability of netting and collateral arrangements has also been an obstacle.

kets, either organized or over the counter, including brokers and other intermediaries.

A number of technical issues in the design and function of instruments and markets should also be addressed, because a lack of standards can often constitute a considerable obstacle to the development and acceptance of

new instruments and markets. These issues include day-count, computation, and payment methods for money and fixed income markets; information systems; and the availability of indices and reliable benchmarks. Wherever possible, these should be compatible with international standards and accepted market practices.

A Direct Role for the Central Bank

The central bank can consider taking a proactive role in developing hedging or complementary markets. Its role might include providing incentives or institutional support to products or markets. Central bank policy and operations will often play a role in spurring the development of markets. For example, monetary policy using open market operations will provide a powerful incentive to traded securities markets and the development of repurchase transactions.

The central bank could also initiate the development of instruments and markets by actually issuing or making a market in instruments such as forwards and options (for example, see Israel's experience in Appendix Box A1). The case for an explicit central bank role is not clear-cut. Arguments supporting an active role include the possibility of market failure (in the sense of multiple equilibrium, inertia, collusion, or coordination failures); relative advantage of the central bank; or the existence of a development cycle, where there is a natural role for the central bank as a catalyst. Moreover, the argument can be made that risks and costs already exist and in many cases are borne by the central bank; the use of tradable instruments simply makes the role of the central bank more transparent and explicit.

However, there are also weighty arguments against the central bank taking a direct role in developing financial markets. It is not a core central bank role, and could be counterproductive in the long term if it displaces or crowds out the private sector or introduces distortions and inefficiencies. There is a risk of failure, with implications for the reputation and credibility of the bank. This direct role adds financial risk and operational risks that require the managing of scarce resources; if they are not managed correctly, failures could be costly.

Given the risks and uncertainties, any direct role for the central bank should be carefully considered and well prepared. If the central bank does decide to play a proactive role, goals should be carefully defined and limited, and the role of the central bank should be delineated and circumscribed from the outset. Milestones should be established so that the central bank role does not become self-perpetuating, and periodic evaluations of market development and the costs and/or profitability of the central bank should be rigorously examined. If safety nets are extended to the private sector, they should be limited in both extent and duration. Costs and incentives should be made explicit, and any incentives should be tied to obligations. Finally, an exit strategy for the central bank should be prepared and strictly adhered to.

Summary

The main points of this appendix can be summarized as follows:

- FX risk hedging should be encouraged to improve the pricing and managing of risk, increase stability at all levels, and improve welfare. For these goals to be achieved, FX variability should be allowed to increase, regulatory and other obstacles to hedging should be removed, and an appropriate environment should be provided.

- The development of complementary financial markets is essential to the development of the FX market and brings additional benefits to the financial system, including greater efficiency, completeness, improved monetary policy transmission, competition, diversification, and operational efficiency.

- The central bank can promote the appropriate environment, assist in establishing the necessary conditions and infrastructure, and take a number of initiatives to help develop FX hedging and complementary markets. In certain cases a direct role for the central bank might be beneficial, but the costs and risks should be carefully considered.

Bibliography

Ahumada, L.A., F. Alarcón, J. Selaive, and J.M. Villena, 2006, "The Development of the Currency Derivatives Market in Chile," *Central Bank of Chile Financial Stability Report* (first half), pp. 69–77.

Allen, Mark, C. Rosenberg, C. Keller, B. Setser, and N. Roubini, 2002, "A Balance Sheet Approach to Financial Crisis," IMF Working Paper 02/210 (Washington: International Monetary Fund).

Ariyoshi, A., K. Habermeier, B. Laurens, I. Ötker-Robe, J. Canales Kriljenko, and A. Kirilenko, 2000, *Capital Controls: Country Experiences with Their Use and Liberalization*, IMF Occasional Paper No. 190 (Washington: International Monetary Fund).

Arvai, Z., 2005, "Capital Account Liberalization, Capital Flow Patterns, and Policy Responses in the EU's New Member States," IMF Working Paper 05/213 (Washington: International Monetary Fund).

Bank for International Settlements (BIS), 2004, "Triennial Central Bank Survey of Foreign Exchange and Derivatives Market Activity in April 2004" (Basel: Monetary and Economic Department). Available via the Internet: www.bis.org/publ/rpfx04/pdf.

Bank of Israel, *Annual Report* (Jerusalem, various issues). Available via the Internet: http://www.bankisrael.gov.il/publeng/publeslf.php?misg_id=12.

Bank of Israel Foreign Currency Department, *Annual Report* (Jerusalem, various issues). Available via the Internet: http://www.bankisrael.gov.il/publeng/publeslf.php?misg_id=27&toptitle1a=Regular%20Publications.

Basel Committee on Banking Supervision, 1996, *Amendment to the Capital Accord to Incorporate Market Risks* (Basel: Bank for International Settlements). Available via the Internet: http://www.bis.org/publ/bcbs24.pdf.

Barrán, F., 2002a, "Política cambiaria y objetivos de inflación en Uruguay" (Exchange Rate Policy and Objectives of Inflation in Uruguay), Banco Central de Bolivia *Revista de Análisis*, Vol. 5 (June). Available via the Internet: http://www.bcb.gov.bo/pdffiles/iniciales/revistas/junio2002/Capitulo3final.pdf.

———, 2002b, "Uruguayan 2002 Financial Crisis Resolution at a Glance," paper presented at the FSAP Seminar on Financial Stability and Development, Washington, June 18.

Begg, D., 1998, "Pegging Out: Lessons from the Czech Exchange Rate Crisis," *Journal of Comparative Economics*, Vol. 26 (December), pp. 669–90.

Ben-Bassat, A., 1995, "The Inflation Target in Israel: Policy and Development" in *Targeting Inflation*, ed. by A. Haldane (London: Bank of England).

Bruno, M., 1997, "Growth, Inflation and Economic Stabilization" (Hebrew) (Jerusalem: Bank of Israel).

———, and L. Meridor, 1991, "The Costly Transition from Stabilization to Sustainable Growth: Israel's Case," in *Lesson of Economic Stabilization and Its Aftermath*, ed. by Bruno and others (Cambridge, Massachusetts: MIT Press).

Bruno, M., and S. Piterman, 1988, "Israel's Stabilization: A Two Year Review," in *Inflation Stabilization: The Experience of Israel, Argentina, Brazil, Bolivia and Mexico*, ed. by Bruno and others (Cambridge, Massachusetts: MIT Press).

Buiter, W., and A. Taci, 2003, "Capital Account Liberalization and Financial Sector Development in Transition Countries," in *Capital Liberalization in Transition Countries: Lessons from the Past and for the Future*, ed. by A. Bakker and B. Chapple (Northampton, Massachusetts: Edward Elgar), pp. 105–41.

Campanero, J., and A. Leone, 1991, "Liberalization and Financial Crisis in Uruguay, 1974–87," in *Banking Crises: Cases and Issues*, ed. by V. Sundararajan and T. Baliño (Washington: International Monetary Fund).

Čapek, A., T. Hlédik, V. Kotlán, S. Polák, and D. Vávra, 2003a, "Developing Consistent Scenarios with the Forecasting and Policy Analysis System," in *The Czech National Bank's Forecasting and Policy Analysis System*, ed. by W. Coats, D. Laxton, and D. Rose (Prague: Czech National Bank).

———, 2003b, "Historical Perspective on the Development of the Forecasting and Policy Analysis System," in *The Czech National Bank's Forecasting and Policy Analysis System*, ed. by W. Coats, D. Laxton, and D. Rose (Prague: Czech National Bank).

Carare, A., A. Schaechter, M.R. Stone, and M. Zelmer, 2002, "Establishing Initial Conditions in Support of Inflation Targeting," IMF Working Paper 02/102 (Washington: International Monetary Fund).

Central Bank of Chile, *Annual Report* (Santiago, various issues). Available via the Internet: http://www.bcentral.cl/eng/funorg/annualreport/.

Céspedes, L.F., and C. Soto, 2005, "Credibility and Inflation Targeting in an Emerging Market: Lessons from the Chilean Experience," *International Finance*, Vol. 8 (Winter), pp. 545–75.

Chan-Lau, J.A., 2005, "Hedging Foreign Exchange Risk in Chile: Markets and Instruments," IMF Working Paper 05/37 (Washington: International Monetary Fund).

Christensen, J., 2004, "Capital Inflows, Sterilization, and Commercial Bank Speculation: The Case of the Czech